The chimes call midnight, just at interlune,
And the daytime talk of the Roman investigations
Was checked by silence, save for the husky tune
The bubbling waters played near the excavations,

And a warm air came up from underground,
And a flutter, as of a filmy shape unsepulchred,
That collected itself, and waited, and looked around:
Nothing was seen, but utterances could be heard:

extract from THOMAS HARDY: '*Aquae Sulis*'

DEAE SVLI MINERVAE
D.D.

ROMAN
BATH
DISCOVERED

Barry Cunliffe

ROUTLEDGE & KEGAN PAUL
London, Boston, Melbourne and Henley

First published in 1971
by Routledge & Kegan Paul plc
39 Store Street, London WC1E 7DD, England
9 Park Street, Boston, Mass. 02108, USA
464 St Kilda Road, Melbourne,
Victoria, 3004, Australia
Broadway House, Newtown Road,
Henley-on-Thames, Oxon RG9 1EN, England
Revised edition 1984
Set in Bembo
and printed in Great Britain by
BAS Printers Limited, Over Wallop, Hampshire

Library of Congress Cataloging in Publication Data

Cunliffe, Barry W.
Roman Bath discovered.

Bibliography: p.
Includes index.
1. Bath (Avon)—Antiquities, Roman. 2. Romans—England—Bath (Avon)
3. England—Antiquities, Roman. I. Title.
DA147.B3C85 1984   936.2'398   83-19119

ISBN 0-7102-0196-6

Contents

List of illustrations

LIST OF ILLUSTRATIONS

LIST OF ILLUSTRATIONS

Preface

Preface to the first edition

My first visit to the Roman baths was memorable. I was fifteen, it was hot, and I was bored. Sitting in one of the alcoves on the south side of the Great Bath, feeling guilty at my lack of enthusiasm for one of Britain's greatest Roman monuments and flicking through the old guide book, I suddenly came upon a photograph taken in the 1880s showing an eighteenth-century building overhanging the then partly excavated baths. Immediately the Roman monument took on a dynamic relationship with the recent past – there was a time nearly sixty years before when the alcove in which I was sitting still lay beneath the Georgian city. Curiosity was awakened.

An examination of the plan showed that instead of looking at a completely known building, the establishment was surrounded by big question marks – Roman walls disappeared behind modern walls and all around lay the word 'unexcavated'. How dare they leave all this unexcavated! But who were they? Then I began to discover the discoverers: Samuel Lysons, Major Davis, James Irvine – the people who in the last 250 years had, like me, looked on the incomplete monument and wanted to know more. By playing on a schoolboy's unsophisticated curiosity the gods of Bath had established a fascination which was to lead to many happy pilgrimages in the years to follow.

My appointment, in 1963, to a lectureship in archaeology at Bristol University brought me close to the town, which had just set up an excavation committee upon which I was invited to serve. Gradually, through a growing familiarity with the structure and by means of a series of limited but intensely satisfying excavations, the major questions began to be answered, but with each solution the fascination of the site grew stronger. No archaeologist can, however, allow himself the luxury of hoarding his results for long. By 1968 a stage had been reached when a definitive publication of the research of the previous five years became desirable. The detailed monograph was prepared and was published in the following year. But a monograph written for a small community of professional archaeologists is at best terse, detailed and close-packed; it can do scant justice to the joy of the subject. Out of this realization has grown the present book. It is an attempt to offer to the general reader a little of the excitement of discovery and a summary of our present state of knowledge. It is my offering to the gods of the place in return for the pleasure they have given me. If it does no more than make the reader want to see the buildings for himself or see them again, it will have served its purpose.

But this is not the end: it is merely the end of one stage in the continuous story of the discovery. As these words are being written, new plans are being proposed for the redevelopment of the nineteenth-century part of the Pump Room complex – plans which will enable vast areas of the western end of the baths to be carefully examined and exposed for visitors to see. The discovery of Roman Bath is, and always will be, a continuing process.

Barry Cunliffe
Southampton
Easter 1969

Preface to the second edition

Not the end indeed! The excavation of the western baths took place, and much more beside. I could hardly have conceived in 1969 that so much could have happened in so short a period: six new excavations about the city; a unique opportunity to examine the very heart of Bath – the centre of the sacred spring; and a three-year campaign of excavation laying bare the central area of the temple precinct. For those of us privileged to take part in the work it has been a memorable period.

The spirit in Bath has changed dramatically in the last decade. The buildings are cleaner and better looked after than ever before (though some of the new additions are barely tolerable), the town seems younger and happier and there is a new awareness of the city's uniqueness. Even more important, the spa, after a sad period of dereliction, is about to be reborn. The immediate prospect for more large-scale excavation in little known areas holds out the strong probability that we may, within the next few years, be able to add significantly to our knowledge of this remarkable city.

Barry Cunliffe
Oxford
May 1983

Acknowledgments

The author wishes to thank the following:

Cambridge University Press for permission to reprint the translation of 'The Ruin' from N. Kershaw, *Anglo-Saxon and Norse Poems* (Cambridge 1922); G. Bell & Sons Ltd. for permission to reprint from J. E. W. Wallis, *The Welding of the Race* (London 1924); and the Thomas Hardy Estate, Macmillan & Co. Ltd., and The Macmillan Company of Canada Limited, for permission to reprint 'Aquae Sulis' from *Collected Poems* of Thomas Hardy.

The photographic illustrations are by David Leigh, E. A. Shore, Mike Rouillard, Nick Pollard and Bob Wilkins with the exception of figs 1 and 61, which are reproduced by permission of the British Museum. Many of the line illustrations are based on artwork originally published by The Society of Antiquaries of London.

1
BEGINNINGS OF ANTIQUARIAN INTEREST

Throughout its two thousand years of life, the town of Bath has always been famous as a great religious centre and for its thermal springs with their curative associations. All the time that society has held these properties in high regard, Bath has been a forcing-ground for cultural development, whether in the Roman period or a thousand years later. In the following chapters, much will be said of the town as a flourishing Roman centre, a development which set the scene for the future. Here we must consider how subsequent society came to regard its origins and how, with an added sophistication, it began to discover them.

Out of the decaying carcase of the Roman town, with its shadowy sub-Roman existence lasting to the time of the famous Battle of Dyrham in A.D. 577, grew a small Christian community of nuns and secular canons said to have been founded by Osric, a sub-king of the Hwicce, in 675. With an endowment of considerable estates outside the town, the monastery flourished and within a hundred years it could be referred to as a *monasterium celeberrimum*. What use was made at this stage of the hot springs is uncertain: it is most unlikely that they were neglected by the community and by 956 'pleasant hot baths' were mentioned in association with the religious buildings. Throughout mid- to late-Saxon times, with the development of constructional techniques, in particular the use of stone, the monastic buildings must have grown in extent and grandeur. Indeed a charter of 957 describes the Church of St Peter as 'built with marvellous workmanship' (*mira fabrica*). It was evidently held in some regard, for on Whit Sunday 973, Edgar was crowned here by Oswald, Archbishop of York, and Dunston, Archbishop of Canterbury, in what can be regarded as a prototype of the present coronation service. The monastery, placed under the control of the Benedictines, continued to flourish together with the secular community clustering round it, which was now important enough to possess a mint. But its Saxon glory came to an end in the troubles of 1088 which followed the death of William Rufus, when a large area of Somerset rose in revolt against the king and, in retaliation, Bath was laid waste.

In July of the destruction year John de Villula, a doctor from Tours who had later become ordained, was consecrated to the see of Somerset, at this stage centred on Wells. The new bishop was evidently interested in the curative waters at Bath and he managed to acquire the entire ruined city from the king, complete with its mint, abbey and springs, later confirming his ownership by paying 500 pounds of silver. Here he soon transferred his see and in about 1090 set about replacing the old Saxon buildings with a large new Norman cathedral more than 100m long, at the same time refitting the hot baths and developing their medicinal use. Under his patronage the religious and cultural life of the town flourished. In the collegiate school which he created, the mediaeval scientist Abélard received his first introduction to scholarship and after travelling and studying widely returned to the quiet of the monastery to complete his famous treatise on the astrolabe. By the middle of the twelfth century, Bath had achieved a world-wide reputation not only for the quality of its scholarship, but for the healing properties of the curative waters, now made available to pilgrims at several different hospitals.

In the atmosphere of enlightened scholarship, it was inevitable that people should enquire into the origins of the town. Who had first discovered the spring, when, and how? This was really part of the widespread desire of mediaeval scholars to know something of their past. Their society was fast reaching a stage of stable maturity but it badly needed roots. There were reputable historians, such as William of Newburgh, who wrote his *Historia Rerum Anglicarum* (*1066–1198*) from the available sources, but what happened before 1066? Apart from Bede, Nennius, the Bible and the classical writers, there was little source material available. It seemed that stalemate had been reached, but about 1135 a cleric from Wales, Geoffrey of Monmouth, announced a major break-through. He had in his possession, he claimed, 'a very old book' from Brittany written in the British tongue and given to him by his friend Walter, Archdeacon of Oxford. This source, he said, formed the basis of his own *Historia Regnum Britanniae*, a major work in which he traced the descent of the British kings from the Trojan Brutus, who landed in Britain at Totnes about 1170 B.C. (when Eli was High Priest) and conquered the island after beating the giants who were at the time in possession. Merging odd half-understood fragments of classical history, biblical events and scraps of legends with much that must be fanciful invention, the book continues in this vein. Whatever the nature of the source material, whether the 'very old book' ever existed, the fact remains that Geoffrey had access to traditions and folk tales since lost. It is a pity that these have been immersed beyond recovery in the mass of glamorous speculative nonsense which his colourful mind must have invented.

In Geoffrey's legendary history, Bath plays a significant part. His story is worth retelling, if only as an example of how important it was to the mediaeval intellect to be provided with origin stories that were well-rounded, readily understandable in human terms and with a touch of the parable. It all begins with a young prince, Bladud, the eldest son of King Lud. To provide him with the kind of liberal education suitable for a king, Lud sent Bladud to study at Athens for eleven years, but there he contracted leprosy (one of the evils of going abroad) and had to be locked away when he returned home.

However, being a young man of spirit, he escaped to a remote part of the country and took up employment as a swineherd in a small village not far from Bath (thus demonstrating a love of liberty at any price and social conscience in keeping his contagious self away from other people). One day, whilst meditating on a hill overlooking Bath, he noticed that his pigs had suddenly rushed down into an alder swamp below, where they began to wallow in the black mud around a spring. It occurred to him that this was an odd thing even for pigs to do in winter, but as he approached he saw that the spring was hot and concluded that the pigs came to enjoy the warm mud. He soon noticed, however, that the mud bath had cured the animals of the sores and scurf from which they had been suffering. Being of an enquiring mind, he decided to see what effect the mud would have on his leprosy: needless to say, he was cured. After some difficulty in persuading his employer that he was the king's son, he eventually returned to his father's court and when, some years later, he succeeded to the throne, he showed his gratitude by building the baths around the spring at Bath.

It is a happy tale, full of romance and sound morals and one which proved popular to the inhabitants of Bath. Indeed, even after the total unreliability of Geoffrey's work had become clear, the story continued to be told with modifications and amendments. One version tells how Bladud built a magnificent city around the baths and lived there into his declining years, until one day he finally succumbed to his delusions of grandeur and decided to fly from the top of Minerva's Temple, with a notable, and fatal, lack of success. Endless variations on the Bladud legend can still be heard in the town.

Like the mythical Bladud, John de Villula was also a victim of his illusions, for the vast cathedral priory which he had begun was far too large for a community the size of Bath, and its construction suffered from various setbacks. Nor were funds readily forthcoming for its upkeep. By the early fourteenth century it was even necessary to hold a general collection throughout the diocese to obtain sufficient money for restoration. Nevertheless, the city continued to thrive as an important wool-producing centre and Leland, writing in the early sixteenth century, was able to state that 'the town hath for a long time syns bene continually most mayntainid by making of clothe'. Towards the end of the fifteenth century Bishop Oliver King decided to replace the old building, now neglected and near collapse, by a completely new construction of considerably shorter length, but forty years later, at the time of the Dissolution, the nave was still without a roof and there was no glass in the windows.

It was partly because of the Dissolution that John Leland, librarian, chaplain and later antiquary to King Henry VIII, began his tours of Britain, for the Dissolution was a time when monastic libraries were being broken up and the manuscripts dispersed. It was also a time of renewed interest in the past, when after a period of speculation and arid academic discussion it was at last realized that more facts were required and the only way to produce them was to go out and look for them. With these two ends in mind, Leland set out on a series of remarkable journeys which were to take him from 1536 to 1542 to complete. Six years of travelling over the inadequate roads of Tudor England was an achievement of some magnitude.

When Leland arrived at Bath he began to study its monuments and buildings in some detail. He describes the gates, the circuit of the wall, 'of no great highth', and notes that no towers survived except at the gates themselves. Then follows an admirable description of carved stones, presumably of Roman date, embedded in the superstructure of the wall:

> There be divers notable antiquitees engravid in stone that yet be sene yn the walles of Bathe betweixt the south gate and the weste gate: and agayn betwixt the west gate and the north gate. The first was an antique hed of a man made al flat and having great lokkes of here as I have in a coine of C. Antius. The secunde that I did se bytwene the south and the north gate was an image, as I tooke it, of Hercules: for he held yn eche hand a serpent. Then I saw the image of a foote man *vibrato gladio & praetenso clypeo*. Then I saw a braunch with leaves foldid and wrethin into Somerset circles. Then I saw ij. nakid imagis lying a long, the one

imbracing the other. Then I saw to antique heddes with heere
as rofelid yn fo. 36 lokkes. Then I saw a greyhound as renning,
and at the taile of hym was a stone engravid with great Romane
letters, but I could pike no sentence out of it. Then I saw another
inscription, but the wether hath except a few lettres clere defacid.
Then I saw toward the west gate an image of a man embracid
with 2. serpentes. I took, it for Laocoon. Betwixt the weste and
the north gate. I saw 2. inscriptions, of wich sum wordes were
evident to the reader, the residew clene defacid. Then I saw the
image of a nakid man. Then I saw a stone having *cupidines &
labruscas intercurrentes.* Then I saw a table having at eche ende an
image vivid and florishid above and beneth. In this table was a
inscription of a tumbe or burial wher in I saw playnly these
wordes: *vixit annos xxx.* This inscription was meately hole but
very diffusely written, as letters for hole wordes, and 2. or 3.
letters conveid in one. Then I saw a. 2 images, wherof one was
of a nakid manne grasping a serpent in eche hand, as I tooke it:
and this image was not far from the north gate. Such antiquites
as were in the waulles from the north gate to the est, and from
the est gate to the south, hath been defacid by the building of
the monastery, and making new waulles.

The description is quite remarkable for its accuracy and perception.
Yet Leland was not content simply to record his observations. He
offered some comment on them, arguing that the blocks were more
likely to be re-used in post-Roman rebuilding than set in place in
the Roman period. He is the first scholar to offer any record of the
antiquities which, though noted on subsequent occasions, gradually
disappeared as the wall was pulled down piece by piece to make way
for new developments.

The town which Leland saw had 'sumwhat decayed' since the
high period of the woollen industry, but nevertheless it could boast
three baths served by mineral waters that 'rikith like a sething potte
continually having sumwhat a sulphureus and sumwhat onpleasant
savor'. The King's Bath in the centre of the town, close to the west

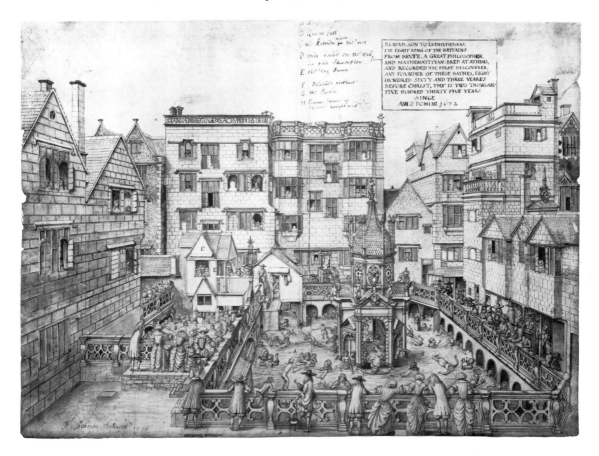

end of the cathedral, was 'very faire and large' and was enclosed by a high wall provided with arches 'for men and women to stand separately yn'. The other two baths were less fashionable. The Cross Bath, for example, was 'much frequentid of people deseasid with lepre, pokkes, scabbes and great aches' whilst the Hot Bath was a minor affair of only seven arches compared with the thirty-two of the King's Bath.

Leland settled down in 1545 to begin to prepare his voluminous notes for publication, but five years later he was certified insane and in 1552 he died, his work unfinished. The notes eventually found their way into the Bodleian Library at Oxford, where they were

1 The focal centre of Bath in the seventeenth and eighteenth centuries was the King's Bath, shown here in remarkable detail in a pen and wash drawing by Thomas Johnson (1675). The King's Bath is immediately above the Roman spring and reservoir.

7

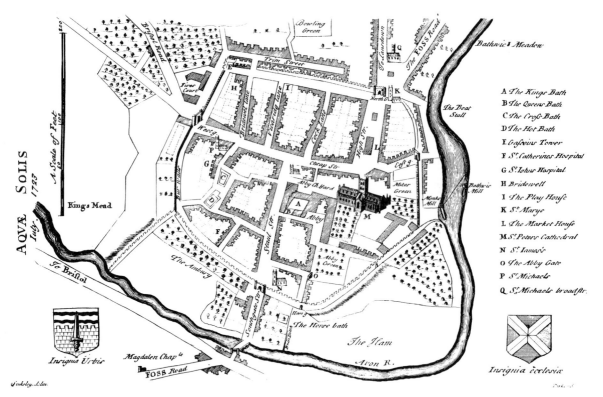

AQVÆ SOLIS
July: 1723

A Scale of Feet

To Bristol

King's Mead

Insignia Urbis

Magdalen Chap.le
FOSS Road

Bristol Road
Bowling Green
Trim Street
River Court
The Gallery
The FOSS Road

A The Kings Bath
B The Queens Bath
C The Cross Bath
D The Hot Bath
E Gascoins Tower
F St Catherines Hospital
G St Johns Hospital
H Bridewell
I The Play House
K St Marys
L The Market House
M St Peters Cathedral
N St James's
O The Abby Gate
P St Michaels
Q St Michaels broad str.

Bathwick Meadow
The Boat Stall
Bathwic Mill

West g.
Friedland Lane
Westrick gate
Cheap Str.
Abby Ch.Yard
Mitre Green

North G.
North g
Broad Str.
Stall St.
High Str.
Cock Lane

The Amhury
The Horse bath
The Ham
Avon R.

Southgate St.
Southgate St.
Hare g
Fraud Str.
Abby Green

Insignia ecclesia

Stukeley delin.

2 Bath in the early eighteenth century: Stukeley's map, showing the town before the work of John Wood completely altered the landscape, gives a clear idea of the town as it would have been throughout much of the mediaeval period.

used freely by those who followed in Leland's footsteps, men such as the equally famous topographer William Camden, but it was not until 1710–12 that *The Itinerary of John Leland* was eventually published under the editorship of Thomas Hearne. Leland's travels had, however, initiated a new era in antiquarian studies: scholars were at last ready to go into the field in search of their raw material.

Leland's visit was followed in the second half of the sixteenth century by the arrival of William Camden. After a detailed examination of the walls he was able to describe several new inscriptions that had not previously been noticed. These he included in *Britannia*, first published in 1586. Ninety years later Dr Thomas Guidott, writing his *A Discourse on Bathe*, was able to add 'two fierce heads, one within the cope of the Wall, and another to the outside thereof hard by'. He also noted 'a Hare running, now lost' and 'An angry man

8

laying hold of a poor peasant, which may be a bold insulting Roman on a poor distressed captivated Briton' and many others. But even by this time sculptures known to exist were fast disappearing. When William Stukeley visited the town in 1724 the walls were still largely intact. He does, however, make the important distinction between what he considers to be original Roman work and the upper part which seems to have been repaired with the ruins of Roman buildings, for, he says,

> the lewis holes are still left in many of the stones; and to the shame of the repairers, many Roman inscriptions, some sawn across to fit the size of the place, are still to be seen, some with the letters towards the city, others on the outside. Most of those mentioned by Mr. Camden and other Authors are still left; but the legend most obscure.

By the middle of the eighteenth century Bath had begun to reap the benefits of its new-found prosperity; but elegant towns needed spacious approaches, which meant that the old mediaeval gates had to be removed, and once the gates were gone, the now functionless walls began gradually to disappear. Occasionally some watch was kept for inscribed blocks, but very few of those recorded by the earlier writers survived. Indeed, apart from an inscription found during the demolition of the Westgate in 1776 and a group of stones recovered from close to the north gate in 1803, most of the Roman stones must have disappeared into the rubble core or footings of the eighteenth-century terraces.

While it is true to say that most of the more obvious archaeological remains found from the sixteenth century onwards were in some way recorded, survival was another matter. Two case histories will suffice to demonstrate the problems. In 1592 two tombstones, one of G. Murrius Modestus, the other to M. Valerius Latinus, were dug up at Walcot along the line of the Roman Fosseway which leads towards the north gate of the city. Presumably they belonged to the first- and second-century cemetery, which is known to have spread along the road in this area. To begin with the stones were taken by a Mr Robert Chambers to his garden near the Cross Bath, there to be commemorated by a new inscription which read:

HAEC.MONVMEN.VIO
LATA.SVLCIS.IN.CA
MP.DE.WALCOT.R. C.
CVLTOR.ANTIQ.HVC.
TRANSTVLIT. AN
VER.INCAR. 1592

Camden saw them on his visit to the town and included an account of them in a later edition of *Britannia*. When Dr Guidott was in Bath in 1673 they still appear to have been in the same place in the north wall of the garden, now belonging to a Mr Crofts. Horsley tells us that in 1725 they were still in position and they were mentioned later, in 1749, by Wood as 'to be seen in the north wall of the garden which makes Chandos Court complete', but in the spate of rebuilding which followed in the second half of the eighteenth century both stones completely disappeared, no doubt for use as hard-core in some near-by structure. By 1791, when Collinson was writing his *History of Somerset*, they were nowhere to be found.

The story of another object has a happier ending. In 1714 or 1715, 'when ye way was mended were Walcot ajacent to the City of Bath', a colossal female head (fig. 116), adorned with a Flavian hairstyle, was found. It, too, must once have belonged to a funerary monument of some kind. A local resident, Francis Child, took charge of it and sent it as a present to his friend Dr Musgrave in Exeter, where it was set up in the porch of his house. In 1859 the head was still there when the Reverend Scarth visited the house to inspect it. A few years later it was removed and returned to the Bath Literary and Philosophical Institution, whence it finally came into the present Roman Baths Museum after the Institution closed down during the Second World War. After 1600 years in the earth and nearly 250 years in private collections, the head is now displayed for all to see.

Interest in the antiquities of the town throughout the sixteenth and seventeenth centuries rested more with visiting scholars than with the local population, for this was a period of rapid development at Bath, a time when the town was busy transforming itself from the smelly squalor of a provincial wool town, which frightened even Queen Elizabeth I away after a very brief visit, into an elegant display of terraces, parades, squares and gardens suitable to be graced by the highest ranks of society. John Wood's description of the transition period, though biased to throw his own architectural achievements into stronger contrast, is not without a certain accuracy. He writes:

> The streets and public ways of the city were become like so many dunghills, slaughter house, and pig-styes: for soil of all sorts, and even carrion, were cast and laid in the streets, and the pigs turned out by day to feed and rout among it; butchers killed and dressed their cattle at their own doors; people washed every kind of thing they had to make clean at the common conduits in the open streets; and nothing was more common than small racks and mangers at almost every door for the baiting of horses.

Even the baths did not appeal to him. They were, he said, 'like so many bear gardens; and modesty was entirely shut out of them; people of both sexes bathing by day and night naked; and dogs, cats, and pigs, even human creatures, were hurl'd over the rails into the water, while people were bathing in it' (figs 1 and 3).

Nevertheless the growing fame of the waters brought illustrious visitors prepared to face these horrors. In Charles I's reign, Queen Henrietta Maria preferred the English springs to those of her native France. Catherine of Braganza, Mary of Modena, Anne of Denmark, they all came, but it was the visit of Princess Anne in 1692 and her return as queen ten years later that provided the final impetus to the town and flung it suddenly to the forefront of genteel acceptability.

It fell to John Wood, a Yorkshireman of enormous vision, to transform the old town (fig. 2). Wood was in love with the classical world, he had learnt his architecture in the Palladian school and was determined to rebuild Bath as a city fit to rival ancient Rome itself. Many of his more ambitious schemes, which were to include Imperial Gymnasia, a Royal Forum and a Grand Circus, were never completed in the romantic form in which he had first conceived them, but even so, much of the spacious grandeur of his first enthusiastic flood managed to survive the parings of social demand and economic necessity. From 1725 to 1754 he toiled, sponsored by local dignitaries and landowners such as Ralph Allen, Dr Gay and the Duke of Kingston, until by the end of his life the town had been totally transformed. Wood was more than just an architect, he was a romantic whose imagination and innate intelligence led him to become deeply involved with the city and its past. Much of this feeling is evident in his book *The History of Bath*, first published in 1749, but he was working at a time when very little was known of the original Roman town and its monuments. A few inscriptions had turned up, but nothing very tangible, nor did his own building works produce much, for he was working for the most part outside the ancient nucleus. In 1738, however, he began work on the Mineral Water Hospital just inside the north wall of the town and much to his delight he soon uncovered part of a Roman building consisting of walls, mosaics and a hypocaust, all of which he recorded and described with great care (fig. 105). As we now know, these remains were probably part of a town house of late Roman date, but to someone of Wood's imagination the find became the ancient Praetorium – the focal centre of the great Roman town. It was not until the year of Wood's death that the first dramatic evidence of Roman public building came to light when the foundations for the Duke of Kingston's Bath, just south of the abbey, exposed the east end of the Roman thermal establishment.

The second half of the eighteenth century saw not only the further extension of the town away from the centre but also the gradual rebuilding of parts of the old nucleus. Gradually discoveries multiplied and gradually polite society began to take notice. Interest in antiquarian matters had reached such a pitch, particularly after the remarkable discoveries made beneath the Pump Room in 1790,

that Samuel Lysons was prepared to devote much of the first volume of his brilliantly illustrated *Reliquiae Romano Britannicae* to the monuments and buildings of the Roman town. It is this awakening of informed interest which Lysons's work typifies, that marks the beginning of our modern understanding.

3 The comforts of Bath by T. Rowlandson. Bathers enjoy a dip in the King's Bath.

2
DISCOVERY OF
THE TEMPLE

The temple, as we now know it, has taken nearly 300 years to discover, and yet there is still an enormous amount hidden beneath the paving of the abbey yard and the adjacent streets and buildings which will probably not see the light of day for hundreds of years to come. The story of the discoveries made so far is a reflection in miniature of the development of nearly three centuries of archaeological thought and method. But it begins with the work of the Roman writer Solinus, who, in the late third century, published *Collectanea rerum memorabilium* – a description of notable phenomena pieced together from hearsay and observation, covering the whole of the Roman Empire. Writing of Britain, he say that there were hot springs 'furnished luxuriously for human use', and 'over these springs Minerva presides and in her temple the perpetual fire never whitens to ash, but as the flame fades, turns into rocky lumps'. There can be very little doubt that he is writing about Bath. The hot springs were famous throughout the Roman world, indeed the second-century geographer Ptolemy calls Bath *Aquae Calidae*. The description provided by Solinus mentions three things: luxurious baths, a temple to Minerva and a curious inflammable stone used on the temple fires.

He was certainly right about the baths and temple, as the following chapters will show, but what of the stone? Some archaeologists have suggested that he was describing Somerset coal, readily available locally. When it burnt, instead of turning into powdery ash like the wood the Romans were accustomed to use, it became cinders. This is a likely enough explanation, particularly in the light of the find made in 1867, of a heap of cinders near the corner of the temple precinct.

The idea of a temple to Minerva situated somewhere in Bath was very much in the minds of the historians and topographers who wrote of the town from the time of Geoffrey of Monmouth onwards,

4 Life-size gilded bronze head of the goddess Minerva found during the digging of a sewer beneath Stall Street in 1727. The head was once crowned with a separate Corinthian helmet and the entire figure would probably have been the cult statue of the temple.

but until the beginning of the eighteenth century nothing was known of the actual building or of its site. It was not unreasonable for the contemporary writers to suggest that it lay beneath the abbey. Even Stukeley, who visited the town as late as 1723, simply followed the earlier tradition. But a few years after Stukeley's visit the first relevant archaeological discovery was made.

The growing awareness of the joys of Bath and its adoption by the fashion-following upper class, created demands for fine building, and for sanitation. Sanitation came first, with the result that a major sewer was laid along Stall Street, throughout the summer of 1727, in a vast trench 4.5–6 m deep. On 12 July, in the mud and rubble at the bottom of the trench, a workman came upon a life-sized gilded bronze head of Minerva, which at some time in the past had been broken from the torso and discarded (fig. 4). The head is a fine piece of competent, if somewhat dull, Roman workmanship, showing Minerva with her hair parted in the middle. The unfinished top to her head suggests that she was originally wearing a detachable Corinthian helmet. There can be no doubt that the statue to which the head belonged would have been of very considerable importance in Roman Bath – it might well have been the cult statue from the temple itself, but of this we can never be sure. It is easy to imagine the reaction of polite society to the discovery – how perfectly correct, they must have thought, that so elegant and classical a piece should have been discovered in Bath, and at the height of the season too. There the matter rested – Minerva had been discovered but not her temple.

The growing popularity and increasing affluence of the spa led the civic authorities to engage in a policy of extensive rebuilding. By 1790 they had decided that the Pump Room, built in 1706 and enlarged in 1751, needed replacement. The well-known architect Thomas Baldwin was appointed to supervise the work and, by the autumn, foundation trenches for the north and west walls had been sunk into the mud and rubble to a depth of four metres, at which a solid Roman pavement was discovered, while the earth above was found to be packed with collapsed Roman masonry. More than seventy major blocks of sculptured and inscribed stone were recovered. There was great excitement, antiquarians poured in from all parts of the country to see the remarkable find, but they were mainly concerned with the sculptures, not with the structural remains in position, which were passed off with the briefest mention. Sir H. Englefield gave a short account to the Society of Antiquaries on 3 March 1791:

> At about twelve feet below the level of the present street
> workmen discovered a pavement of large stone with steps
> fronting to the east. Of this pavement enough was not laid open
> to discover the form or size of the building to which it belonged.
> It appeared to extend under Stall Street. On it the foundation of
> the present new building is laid, and it will of course be for a
> long time covered from future investigation.

Englefield was right: it was not until 1964 that the area was again excavated, showing, exactly as he had recorded it, the eighteenth-century footing resting directly upon the Roman work. In the disturbed soil of the eighteenth-century foundation trenches, the recent excavation also uncovered a number of wine bottles, lying where they had been discarded by the workmen, or by the visiting archaeologists.

Englefield was not the only visitor to publish an account of the work. Governor Pownall was there at the time and wrote a similar description a few years later, together with notes of other finds turning up along the line of the north walls. There were also many other derivative accounts, most of them illustrating and describing, in varying degrees of accuracy, the great sculptured blocks. All the early work was, however, surpassed when in 1813 Samuel Lysons produced his first volume of *Reliquiae Romano Britannicae* – a brilliantly illustrated and highly accurate description of each of the carved and inscribed stones (figs 5 and 20). Lysons's book is still a standard work, particularly as several of the stones mentioned have since been lost. Nor was he satisfied simply to describe what he saw. He also offered

5 During the rebuilding of the Pump Room in 1790 more than seventy sculptured stones were found, many of them belonging to the temple. Although several antiquaries saw them and produced illustrations of varying quality it was not until 1813 that Samuel Lysons published the first accurate account. Compare with fig. 14.

THE PORTICO OF THE TEMPLE OF MINERVA AT BATH RESTORED.

a reasoned reconstruction of some of the monuments, showing, for example, that many of the fragments belonged to the main front elevation of a remarkable Corinthian temple, the pediment of which depicted a glowering Gorgon's head – this was, without any doubt, the Temple of Minerva.

The discoveries of 1790 had shown two things: that the temple was not near the abbey, but lay somewhere to the north or west of the spring in the region of the Pump Room, and that it was in style a purely classical composition worthy of a place in Rome. Yet there was a distinctly local flavour about its pediment: the Gorgon, in classical mythology always female, was depicted here as a male and a Celtic male at that. What Baldwin's labourers had uncovered was a perfect example of the conflation between a Roman and native deity. The Roman half was Minerva, the local component of the god or goddess Sulis mentioned many times on inscriptions found in various parts of the town. Thenceforth the temple must be ascribed to Sulis Minerva. Again the excitement abated, the new Pump Room was completed (but not by Baldwin, who had quarrelled with the city authorities) and the temple sculptures were available for all to see. Bath settled down in its Regency complacency to preen itself and attempt to maintain its allure in the face of competition from the new-fangled sea-water bathing now indulged in by trend-setting members of the leading families.

Nineteenth-century Bath managed to resist, as it did until recently, new building styles, whether good or bad, but the surge of the Gothic revival did not completely wash over the city. The abbey, for example, was recognized as a worthy Gothic monument suitable for renovation and it was to suffer first, in 1833, at the hands of G. P. Manners and later, between 1864 and 1871, under the direction of Sir Gilbert Scott, who delegated the work to his Clerk of Works, James Thomas Irvine. Irvine, a meticulous man with all the accuracy and skill of a Gothic restorer, immediately fell in love with the city and its past. In his seven years at Bath he amassed volumes of notes on all aspects of the city's history, addressed learned societies and wrote articles for newspapers and national journals. But what is more important, he was an archaeologist of the highest quality, whose questioning mind and accuracy of observation and recording set him well above the vast majority of his contemporaries.

In the year of his arrival, 1864, the old White Hart Inn, on the west side of Stall Street opposite the Pump Room, was derelict.

DISCOVERY OF THE TEMPLE

Assessing the 1790 discoveries, Irvine correctly decided that the temple podium probably lay beneath the hotel and, with a Mr Bates, obtained leave to excavate in the cellars, apparently in the hope of finding a marble floor. No marble floor was discovered, but instead they exposed the solid mass of Roman concrete upon which the temple had stood, the first time that the podium had ever been recorded. A few years later the superstructure of the inn was demolished and between 1867 and 1869 reconstruction began. Irvine, arming himself with a free pass to visit the works whenever he liked, was constantly in the trenches scribbling measurements on odd mud-spattered scraps of paper and old envelopes, jotting down memos of the principal discoveries in his diaries and in the evenings drawing up fair copies of records. This remarkable collection of papers is now preserved in the Bath Reference Library, mostly mounted up in scrap-book fashion by Irvine himself – evidently he couldn't bear to throw away the smallest scrap of paper, however crumpled or dirty.

Working throughout the winter of 1867–8 he was able to record with great accuracy the temple podium (which he had seen three years earlier), a mass of concrete scarred by innumerable pits and disturbances, from which the facing blocks had been removed at a much earlier date, presumably in the Saxon or mediaeval period (fig. 6). Around the podium, on the north and west, he recognized the walls of the colonnade surrounding the temple precinct, and beyond these he noted gravel layers which he considered were probably roads. The work on the foundations of the Grand Pump Room Hotel was completed early in 1868 and by the beginning of the next year the superstructure was almost finished. In March, however, a tunnel was dug beneath Stall Street to join the cellars of the new building with those of the Pump Room. Again Irvine was there finding walls, Roman window-glass and parts of colonnettes and noting them all with his customary diligence.

In three years he had seen and recorded most of the temple podium and much of the precinct around it to an accuracy of $\frac{1}{4}$in., tying his measurements to detailed plans of the new structure, but apart from several lengthy newspaper reports and a passing reference

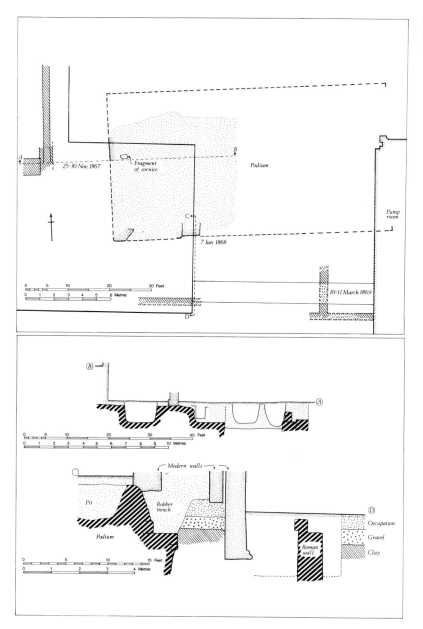

6 Details of the temple podium recorded by J. T. Irvine between 1867–9. (Redrawn after Irvine.)

in a single article, he did not publish his results. It was left to the great Roman scholar, Francis Haverfield, to offer a cursory summary of the Irvine manuscripts in his description of Roman Bath, published forty years later in the *Victoria County History of Somerset*. Haverfield's scathing and grossly unfair assessment of Irvine's work was that it was both inaccurate and fanciful – a description which could hardly be further from the truth, but one which deflected later archaeologists from seriously reconsidering the Irvine records for almost sixty years.

Irvine's reconstruction work on the abbey contributed indirectly to the discovery of the sacred spring and reservoir which was to astound the archaeological world in 1879. Earlier, in 1871, he had discovered, apparently by accident, the massive Roman outfall drain, now known to lead excess water from the spring. But after clearing part of it he was forced to abandon the work and shortly afterwards left Bath for another contract.

Fortunately, during his stay in Bath, Irvine had befriended a local builder, Richard Mann, who was later employed by the City Engineer, Major Charles Davis, to carry out much of the initial clearance of the drain and reservoir. Naturally Mann wrote regularly to his friend Irvine, describing the progress of the work and, characteristically, Irvine preserved every letter. These letters are of very considerable importance for the details they provide of the progress of the excavations and of discoveries otherwise unpublished. They are written in the true tradition of Victorian letter writing, sometimes expansive and often engaging, particularly in the light they throw on the friendship between the two men. On 10 May 1878, for example, Mann writes:

> In shifting a bit of earth from alongside one of them [a stone] I disturbed a frog's last resting place. . . . With great respect to his memory, as he must have been so very much my Senior I preserved what little I could find of him (though I use the Masculine Gender I take no oath on the point). . . . Besides this there is sacred to him a $\frac{1}{2}$ bucket of the adjacent earth reserved for further search in the hopes of finding more of him.

Charming stories they might exchange, but even so each letter begins 'Dear Sir' and ends 'Yours very truely'.

It was in 1878 that Major Davis, worried by the leakage of water from the King's Bath and hoping to improve the drainage there-abouts, employed Mann to open up the Roman drain from the point where Irvine had found it towards the King's Bath. This meant tun-nelling along the line of the largely collapsed drain, barely 1m wide, 6m below ground – a difficult enough job at any time, but without electric light and in the face of a constant stream of hot mineral water, becoming hotter and more persistent the nearer the tunnellers approached the King's Bath, it must at times have been intolerable. Eventually, within a metre or so of what is now known to be the east wall of the Roman reservoir, it was decided to abandon the west-ward advance and, raising the level of the tunnel floor to facilitate drainage, to turn north. It was only then that Mann discovered that they were gradually converging on the massive and well preserved Roman wall running almost parallel to the tunnel on the west side. Excitement mounted as they followed the wall to its north-east cor-ner and then began to tunnel its north face, finding a well-built door in the centre served by a flight of steps. They were now directly beneath the footings of an eighteenth-century wall of the Pump Room and were digging through mud containing massive blocks of stone from the collapsed Roman buildings. Mann writes to Irvine:

> we have been so hindered by the large stone block in our way, which we are obliged to saw up, using it for pillars in front of the Roman wall, about 5ft. apart to support the foundation which overhangs it . . . then in line with it we had another nearly 5ft. long resting partway on the steps . . . you may just imagine what it was to undermine, clear out side, and drag it out in our small culvert.

Some of Mann's stone supports can still be seen *in situ* within the temple precinct.

A little more work on the west side of the enclosure finally established that the Roman reservoir with its rectangular enclosure wall lay exactly beneath the King's Bath. By 9 November, after ten months of exacting work under Major Davis's direction, Mann was beginning to show signs of irritation with his employer. He writes:

> Mr. Davis was down below with us on Tuesday last. He only came to the bottom of the hole and looked right and left, I pointed out the wall opposite to him, he at once took it as a support of his theory that the niches in present Kings Bath are Roman work, but I couldn't agree with him. This is the first time he has been below since a cursory visit with his clerk just as we broke through the 3ft Roman wall . . . he caught cold then, he says, and has not been able to get rid of it since.

Local enthusiasm was by now high; Davis had the King's Bath drained and soon after the floor was ripped up and the excavation of the Roman reservoir began (fig. 7). Immediately the excavators came upon a raft of puddled clay which had served as a foundation for the mediaeval buildings, but once through this they found themselves in a roughly octagonal enclosure, lined with sheets of lead, which surrounded the fissures in the bedrock through which the sacred hot spring issued at the rate of a third of a million gallons a day. Amid the rubble and mud choking the reservoir lay a remarkable array of votive offerings thrown into the waters by the Romans as an act of piety to the goddess Sulis Minerva, or in support of a wish. Fortunately, Major Davis stopped short of digging into these crucial deposits leaving them intact for us to examine 100 years later.

The discoveries were widely reported in the newspapers and in papers read before learned societies, but before adequate records could be made Davis had the lead stripped from the reservoir and sold 'to furnish sinews for the excavations'. Immediately afterwards the reservoir was floored across with a concrete raft supported on arches, leaving only a small trap-door to allow a treacherous descent into the almost unbearable atmosphere of the Roman cistern below. Until 1979 this floor served as the base of the King's Bath.

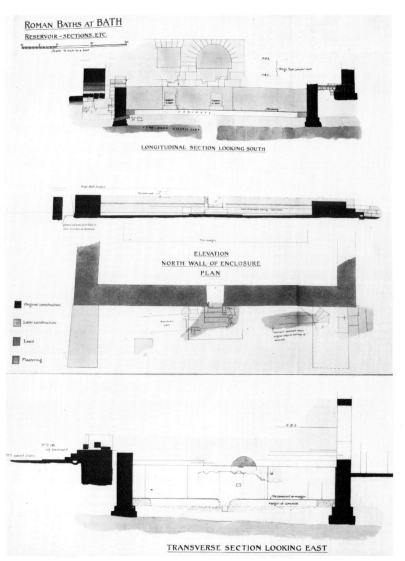

ROMAN BATHS AT BATH
RESERVOIR - SECTIONS, ETC.

LONGITUDINAL SECTION LOOKING SOUTH

ELEVATION
NORTH WALL OF ENCLOSURE
PLAN

Original construction

Later construction

Lead

Plastering

TRANSVERSE SECTION LOOKING EAST

7 Richard Mann, a builder in Bath, was employed during the uncovering of the sacred spring in 1878 and later during the excavation of the baths. He was a fine draughtsman and recorded meticulously everything he exposed. One of his drawings, reproduced here, shows details of the sacred spring. Until excavation began in 1979 his was the only surviving record.

A storm of protest immediately followed but it was too late. Apart from the objects themselves and a series of useful drawings made by Mann, everything was sealed and remained virtually impossible to see until a new programme of work began in 1979.

Davis continued sporadically to excavate the temple area, particularly between 1893 and 1895 when, having completed his work on the Baths (see pp. 99–105), he removed the cellar floors beneath the eighteenth-century Pump Room north of the reservoir and excavated the soil down to the Roman floor levels. This was at the time when the Pump Room extension was being erected. Although he did not realize it, he had uncovered much of the temple precinct, part of the sacrificial altar and most of the main entrance to the temple complex. At the time very little attention was paid to the remains which, it must be admitted, were unimpressive compared with the great baths exposed a decade before. In the end the cellar floors were replaced on a shuttering, leaving the temple features beneath gradually to silt up, totally unrecognized and largely unplanned. The end of the major period of exploration of both the baths and temple came in 1908, when Haverfield wrote a full summary of the Roman town in the *Victoria Country History of Somerset*. Thereafter Bath slept for half a century, but its dramatic monuments could not pass unnoticed for long. In 1955 Professor Ian Richmond reminded the academic world of their importance by publishing, with Professor J. M. C. Toynbee, a full account of the temple façade, but even then he had to admit that the exact position of the temple was unknown. Four years later the Grand Pump Room Hotel, the building of which Irvine had so lovingly watched, was demolished to make way for the new Arlington House. The pace of rebuilding was not as leisurely as in Irvine's day. Modern machinery and the high cost of labour meant that the rescue workers, under the direction of Mr W. Wedlake, had little time to record the exposed Roman features before they were gouged away and concrete was poured in, those Roman structures which still survived again disappearing from view. To echo Englefield – they will, of course, be for a long time covered from future investigation.

The growing awareness of the threat of modern building techniques to the preservation or recovery of archaeological material led to the formation, in 1963, of the Bath Excavation Committee. The overriding responsibility of the Committee was, of course, to excavate and record sites scheduled for redevelopment, but alongside the rescue work a programme of research was planned. The first job was to examine the temple as fully as the overburden of recent buildings and streets allowed. To begin with, many months were spent in the Bath Reference Library of the Society of Antiquaries in London, sifting through wads of manuscript notes, letters, newspaper cuttings, plans and occasional published accounts. Much that was new emerged, particularly from the notes of Thomas Irvine and the plans of Richard Mann, and when eventually the facts were reduced to a single plan, the shape and extent of the temple complex began to emerge as a piece of civic planning far more likely to be found in the towns of Gaul than here in Britain, on the fringes of the Roman world.

The next step involved examining the surviving parts of the Roman building hidden now in cellars and behind the façades of the museum. With this stage partially complete and the details planned, the work of excavation could begin, each trench being designed to answer a specific set of questions. Irvine's records had provided us with the western limits of the temple, while the accounts of 1790 suggested that the steps flanking the east front lay somewhere in the western cellars of the Pump Room close to Stall Street. It was imperative to find them for reasons which will become clear in the next chapter. Working from hints in the 1790 account, a single trial trench was dug through the cellar floor and eventually, 2m down, the lowest step of the temple was uncovered, worn by the tread of innumerable Roman feet. It was a satisfying moment. Standing on the step, 4.6m below the modern city, provided a rare occasion for evocative, rambling thoughts about what it would have been like to stand on this spot 1,600 years earlier, what sounds, what light, what movements. Suddenly the illusion was shattered: from high above in the street a Salvation Army band began to play 'Hark, the Herald Angels Sing': it was Christmas Eve.

The next year, 1965, the work was extended by cutting a single trench along a 2.5m wide cellar which lay beneath the north part of the Pump Room. Work was difficult and cramped with only 0.6m baulks between the trench edge and the cellar walls. The tons of mud and rubble removed had to be got rid of in adjacent cellars. Everything had to be done beneath the intense heat of glaring arc-lamps, with pumps continually at work to remove surface water (figs 8 and 9). To volunteers accustomed to work in the open air the conditions

8 Trial trench in the cellars beneath the Pump Room, dug in 1965. This exploratory work showed the temple precinct to be extremely well preserved 2m below the cellar floor.

9 The trial excavation beneath the Pump Room in the 1960s exposed a remarkable series of Roman structural details. In July 1965 one of the corners of the sacrificial altar was found lying in the mud (see fig. 24).

were at least novel. The rewards, however, were considerable, for not only was the floor of the temple precinct found to be largely intact, but above it lay a mass of collapsed Roman debris including several sculptured blocks, all closely stratified in undisturbed layers of black organic soil formed in the late- and sub-Roman period.

For reasons of safety the trench was dug in three separate sections, leaving 0.6m baulks between so that each could be refilled before the next was cut. The middle section was the last to be dug, and because a modern, somewhat leaky, sewer crossed close to one of the cross baulks the end was left slightly battered and ragged by a squeamish excavator. One noble lady, however, accepting that such untidiness was bad archaeological practice, braved the sewer and carefully began to cut back the end to a regular vertical face. Within a few minutes she had exposed the surface of a statue base inscribed in Latin with the words: 'To the goddess Sulis, Lucius Marcius Memor, augurer, gave this gift' (fig. 8). The block, standing in its original position on the floor of the precinct, had been hidden by a layer of soil less than five cm thick – a tale of virtue rewarded!

DISCOVERY OF THE TEMPLE

For the next two years limited excavation within the cellars continued to fill in details of the temple plan as well as providing more sculptured stones, some of them belonging to monuments already known. Beside the straightforward excavation some considerable time was spent examining the area of the temple precinct uncovered in 1895 by Davis beneath the Pump Room. He had refloored the cellar afterwards with a concrete raft between 1m and 1.5m above the Roman surface, and had provided two small manholes for access. It is difficult to describe the conditions between the two floors: the air was filled with steam from the spring, water constantly flowed across the area and everything was dripping, sodden and rotten. The average temperature, about 43°C, was increased by the heat of the arc lamps which it was necessary to provide. The Roman features which Davis had exposed were now covered with mud lying several centimetres thick below pools of stagnant water, and at intervals pillars of earth and rubble had been left to support the superstructure of the building above. Hell, as it was known to the excavators, was not exactly an idyllic setting for excavation but after a total of four weeks' work by a team of six, working eight hours a day, the most amazing details of the temple precinct and entrance were gradually pieced together.

By 1968 all the exploration that could conveniently be undertaken in the constricted space available had been completed. It was clear to us that if a more extended programme of excavation, combined with display, was to be undertaken, extensive structural work would be necessary beneath the Pump Room to prepare the way. A plan was put forward but was rejected. It was against this background that I wrote, in the first edition of this book,

The Temple of Sulis Minerva is still totally unavailable to visitors, except for some of its sculptures which are now displayed in the museum attached to the baths. Excavation, however, has shown that much of the precinct and surrounding monuments are preserved in a remarkable state 15 to 20 ft below the Pump Room, Abbey Yard and Stall Street (now in this sector a pedestrian precinct). While it must be admitted that full excavation would be a costly and difficult business, given sufficient financial support at least half of the entire temple area on the north side of the reservoir could be uncovered and presented to visitors beneath modern buildings and paving in much the same way as the east baths are now displayed underground. The fragmentary monuments now in the museum could then be reconstructed in their original positions along with the masses of sculptured stone which would inevitably be found. In fact most of the Roman town centre could be exposed 20 ft beneath its modern counterpart in a most dramatic and unique setting.

This is by no means idle pipe-dreaming; the remains are there and all that is needed is the vision, the good will and a substantial sum of money. If, however, public interest continues to increase at its present phenomenal rate it can only be a matter of time before a project on this scale is undertaken.

Eight years later, following local government reorganization, I received a phone call from the newly appointed Director of Leisure Activities, Ray Barratt. His message was brief: he had just read the book, there were now those in Bath with the vision necessary to proceed, and we should meet to talk about it! It was the beginning of one of the most exciting programmes of excavation Bath has ever experienced.

To see the work through a new organization, the Bath Archaeo-logical Trust, was set up and in 1978 the first trial trench was dug in the Pump Room cellars to demonstrate the archaeological poten-tial and to explore the structural problems raised by further work. With the aid of consulting engineers, Manders, Raikes and Marshall, plans were then drawn up for underpinning the Pump Room. The scheme involved building a new supporting wall on the north wall of the Roman enclosure around the spring so that steel beams could be inserted, between this wall and the existing north wall of the Pump Room, to take the weight of the Pump Room floor, thus allowing

the cellar walls beneath to be demolished. In this way an area of some 3000 sq m was made available for excavation, the space to the south of the new south wall becoming an access corridor allowing visitors to view the spring from close quarters.

While plans were in preparation, tragedy struck – a young child died of amoebic meningitis. She had been swimming in the baths, and when the spring water was tested, it was found to be contaminated. Immediately all the baths (including the Roman Bath) were drained and all supplies of spring water were cut off while experts met to consider the problem. The contamination lay in the almost inaccessible reservoir beneath the King's Bath, which Major Davis had created by roofing the Roman reservoir with a concrete raft. In the autumn of 1979 the reservoir was drained and ventilated so that a detailed exploration could be made. Engineers, medical experts and archaeologists together descended into the intensely hot, humid and contaminated chamber, seeing, for the first time in 100 years, the massive Roman walls covered in orange-brown silt and slime. For all of us it was a vividly memorable experience.

The results of the survey were quite clear: the nature of the spring was such that there was little chance of ever being able to sterilize the reservoir chamber. The only option was to tap a fresh supply of pure water from well below ground. But the survey had revealed an additional and totally unsuspected problem. The supporting walls which Major Davis had built across the spring, and his underpinning of the south wall of the Pump Room, had subsided to such an extent that major cracks had begun to appear and serious instability had been created. The only solution was to remove the concrete raft and the sagging supports so that the foundations could be consolidated. Now since the foundations were bedded on undisturbed archaeological deposits of the greatest interest, it meant that a rescue excavation had first to be undertaken. Thus it was that in December 1979, after Davis's concrete raft had been taken away, a new programme of archaeological survey and excavation began in the spring almost exactly 100 years after Davis had ceased digging (figs 10 and 11).

10 The excavation of the sacred spring in December 1979. The arched recesses (centre top) are part of the mediaeval King's Bath. The concrete floor, put in by Major Davis in 1878, has been removed exposing the wall of the polygonal Roman reservoir. The main spring rises in the centre (in front of the table) where the pump stands.

11 Excavations in the sacred spring in December 1979. All the sediment excavated from the reservoir was sieved to ensure that no votive offering was missed.

Within the first day it became clear that Davis had barely touched the significant archaeological deposits. True, he had cleared the reservoir to the Roman tile and concrete surround, removing tons of mud and rubble but, whether by accident or design, he had left, largely intact, the collapsed roof of the Roman reservoir and sealed beneath it, a thick deposit of sand containing the offerings thrown into the spring in the Roman period by suppliants at Sulis Minerva's shrine. The task of the archaeologist was to study the structural history of the Roman reservoir and to remove as much of the stratified deposit as was necessary for the underpinning of the eighteenth-century walls to be carried out.

The excavation was as difficult as it was fascinating. Crucial to the work was the efficiency of the powerful pump used to draw off

34

the constant flow of the spring water: everything depended on its efficiency. Working in the heat of the spring, in protective overalls, wearing face masks and helmets, and usually with the aid of artificial light, one hardly noticed the mid December weather and the shortness of the daylight hours: we arrived in the dark at 7.30 in the morning and left again in the dark at 6.30 at night! Isolated in a world apart, dominated by the ever-present natural force of the spring, we worked in awe of the waters and of the power they had exerted over the minds and lives of the countless pilgrims who in Roman times regarded this place as within direct communication with the gods of the underworld.

The spring lay open throughout 1980 while the structural problems were considered, bore holes driven and the underpinning got underway. Further limited excavation in December clarified the outstanding archaeological problems. Finally in November 1981, after the underpinning had been completed, a filter bed of sand and gravel was laid in the spring, partly to protect the untouched archaeological deposits and partly to prevent the force of the water from bringing up sand from beneath the footings as had happened for the last century. We had excavated a thickness of about 1.5m of silt from half the area of the reservoir – between a sixth and a quarter of what was there before we began. That so much was left untouched was deliberate policy to ensure that future generations of archaeologists have sufficient of this unique deposit to re-examine when they are ready again to do so.

By Easter 1981 the structural work beneath the Pump Room had been completed (fig. 12) and the programme of systematic excavation could at last begin in full sight of a constant flow of visitors. The intricacy of the excavation and the fact that there were no pressures to finish by a particular time, allowed work to proceed at an unusually gentle pace, until, by January 1983, the last vestiges of soil had been removed and the temple precinct was visible again for the first time in 1500 years. The insertion of permanent walkways for visitors, together with the addition of display material, was the final operation before the precinct could be opened to visitors as part

of the Roman Baths and museum complex in April 1983: our hopes and aspirations, expressed in the first edition of this book written thirteen years previously, had at last been realized!

But this is not quite the end of the story for on 18 May 1983 a new angled bore hole, sunk to tap the spring deep beneath the surface well below the contaminated spring head, struck a copious supply of pure mineral water, thus giving the spa the potential of a completely new lease of life. It is perhaps symbolic that the new spring head lies close beside Minerva's temple!

12 To prepare the way for the temple precinct excavation the cellar walls beneath the Pump Room were removed as new steel beams were inserted.

3

THE TEMPLE AND ITS PRECINCT

As the result of the accurate observation and recording undertaken by archaeologists for a quarter of a millennium, the main elements of the temple can now be described (fig. 13). The temple building itself was arranged astride the main east-west axis of the building complex and placed in the centre of a large colonnaded courtyard, 53m by 74m. In front of the temple on the same axis lay the open-air sacrificial altar. The sacred spring and reservoir, the very reason for the existence of Bath, lay in the south-east corner of the temple precinct, immediately south of the altar and so arranged that a north–south visual axis was created from the main hall of the Baths to the south, across the spring, to the altar itself. These, then, are the bare bones of the arrangement but, as will become apparent later, the whole conception was richly ornamented with elaborate subsidiary monuments to enliven, improve and excite.

The temple building (figures 14–22)

Although it is very difficult to get at the temple, most of which lies deep beneath Stall Street, those parts of it that we have been able to examine, together with observations made in the past, show that the building was of two major periods: the original temple put up at the end of the first century A.D. and an extension added some time later, probably in the second half of the second century or a little later. The original building was constructed on a podium of hard concrete rubble about 9m wide and in the order of 14m long, faced with blocks of free-stone. Originally the surface of the platform, about 1.5m above the surrounding level, would have been reached by a flight of steps built against the east end, but details are at present obscure.

The discoveries of 1790 included six large blocks of stone belonging to the richly decorated triangular pediment which formed the central element of the main front. Just enough of the original

13 Plan of the temple precinct seen here in relation to the baths, to the south, and the corner of another monumental building to the east.

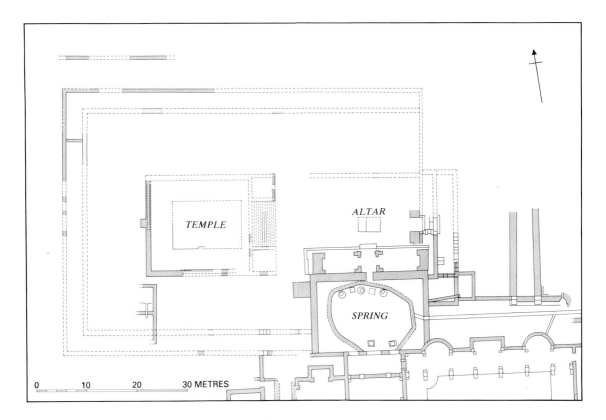

14 Reconstruction of the temple front. Compare with Lysons's reconstruction (fig. 5).

surved to allow the entire composition to be pieced together and another block found in 1982 adds further useful details (fig. 16). It is, without a doubt, one of the most dramatic pieces of sculpture from the whole of Roman Britain (figs 14–17). In the centre, held aloft by two very classical-looking winged Victories, is a circular shield bordered by oak wreaths, from the centre of which glowers a Gorgon's head. Although the Gorgon is normally a female in classical mythology, here in Bath, as we have already mentioned, he is shown in the guise of a male with the wedge-shaped nose, the lentoid eyes, moustaches and beetling brow of a Celtic god. His fierce upstanding hair merges into wings and serpents as he stares, in no way incongruously, from his classical surroundings. The winged Vic-

15 Parts of the temple pediment and its cornice, found in 1790 when the Pump Room was built, have been reassembled in the Roman Baths Museum.

41

tories perch precariously upon globes, while beyond them, in the corners of the pediment, are figures thought possibly to be tritons, but too little of them now survives to be sure. Below the shield, filling the spaces between its curved lower edge and the drapery of the Victories, are two helmets, one in the form of a dolphin's head, the other providing a perch for a rather startled owl, rooted to the ground by two hands clasping his wings. Both owl and dolphin are attributes closely linked to Minerva.

It is difficult to escape from the view that the Bath Gorgon is

16 Another block from the pediment was found in the excavation of 1982. It belongs immediately to the left of the Gorgon's head (fig. 15) and shows the hand and one of the wings of the left-hand Victory. 70cm across.

17 The centre-piece of the temple pediment. It shows a male version of a Gorgon's head – a superb example of the conflation of Roman and Celtic art styles.

18 One of the highly decorated cornice blocks from the main temple front.

a visual conflation of the classical Gorgon and a manifestation of the Celtic god or goddess Sulis, who is presented here perhaps in the guise of a sun god. The purely classical surroundings and the attributes of Minerva are, however, a strong reminder of the Roman take-over. The pediment is truly a brilliant merging of the two traditions and provides a fitting centrepiece for the temple dedicated to Sulis Minerva.

If the survival of a large part of the pediment was fortunate, so too was the discovery in 1790 of a number of blocks belonging to the cornice which surrounded it (figs 15 and 18). All the sections now remaining are richly decorated with a continuous band of flowers, leaves, tendrils and bunches of fruit, reminiscent in some degree of work found in Northern and Eastern Gaul. Whether or not the Bath cornice was carved by a Gaulish craftsman must remain an open question while so little is known of the origin and development of local British schools of sculpture, but the similarities between the Bath and Gaulish work are certainly suggestive of close contact. Interesting proof that the cornice did in fact belong to the Gorgon's head pediment was provided by one of the blocks from the raking cornice, that is the cornice lying above one of the sloping upper edges of the pediment. The lower edge of this particular block had been cut at an angle to join the surface of the horizontal cornice along the bottom of the pediment; the angle matched that of the lower corner of the pediment.

Below the pediment would have been a frieze and architrave supported by the columns of the temple front. The frieze is completely unknown, but in such surroundings it must have been elaborately decorated. There is very little of the architrave, except for one small fragment, again found in 1790, inscribed with the well-cut letters]VM, 11cms high (fig. 19). It is very tempting to see this as the end of the word TEMPLVM, but unfortunately unless more of it is found the matter will remain unresolved.

The columns of the main temple front are known from pieces discovered in 1790, in the spring in 1879 and again in the temple precinct in 1982 (figs 20 and 21). The massive, simple Attic bases

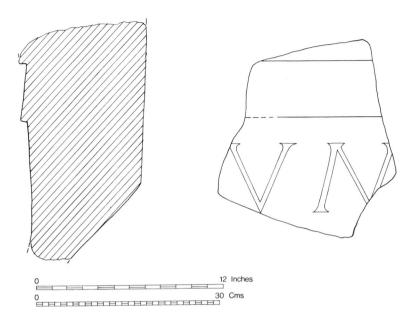

0   12 Inches

0   30 Cms

(1.14m in diameter), fluted shafts and elaborately carved Corinthian capitals, rising to a height of about 8m, are grandiose monumental architecture of a kind very rare in Britain. Again, stylistic considerations suggest the hand of an Eastern Gaulish master craftsman. Knowing the proportions of the columns there can be little doubt that the temple was tetrastyle, i.e. there were four columns supporting the pediment. This fact, taken together with the width of the pediment, suggests that the whole front would have been about 9m wide which exactly fits the estimated width of the podium.

The columns preserved from 1790 were all hollowed out from behind leaving a skin barely 15cms thick. This was thought to imply that the surviving fragments were from half or three-quarter columns set back against the wall of the cella, rather than from the main columns of the temple front. However, it is now clear that most of the sculptured fragments found in 1790, including the Gorgon's head pediment, were thinned down soon after discovery by sawing off the backs. This kind of treatment was quite normal in the eighteenth century and we may reasonably suppose that the hollowing of the

45

20 The columns of the temple were of the Corinthian order, with fluted drums and elaborate foliate capitals. The single surviving capital from the temple was carved in two pieces and shows an unusual leafy tendril growing up onto the *abacus*. Part of the base of the column has been cut away to allow a low balustrade or railing to butt up to it. The illustration is by Samuel Lysons.

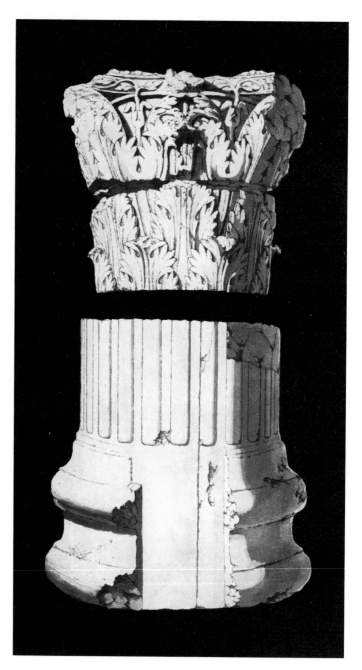

columns took place at the same time. That all the fragments found in 1879 and 1982 were of solid columns adds support to this view. This means that there is no longer any reason to argue for a pseudo-peripteral arrangement (i.e. half columns set against a cella).

How, then, were the different elements of the original temple laid out? The simplest explanation would be to suppose that the plan was *prostyle*, that is the four-column front was separated from a sim-

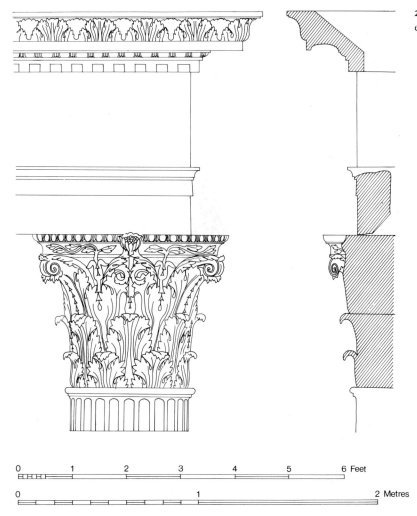

21 Reconstruction of the entablature of the temple.

22 The steps of the temple
exposed in 1981 immediately
against the west wall of the
Pump Room. The steps were
very worn and had been partly
cut back so that new treads could
be added.

ple cella by a short porch (or *pronaos*). Such an arrangement would fit quite well with the proportions of the podium. Whether the actual plan was like this, or one of the more complex variants, we are unlikely to know until the entire podium has been excavated, and even then the crucial evidence may well have been destroyed.

The early temple was doubled in size, probably in the late second century. This seems to have been done by leaving the original structure intact and enclosing it within a surrounding ambulatory incorporating a monumental east front. How the ambulatory was treated we cannot say: it may have been little more than a raised walkway around the original building but the revetting wall could have supported columns and there may even have been a lean-to roof resting against the temple sides. The new front was an ingenious construction designed so as to leave the original façade entirely visible when viewed from the east. Immediately in front of it was a new flight of stone stairs flanked on either side by small rooms, very probably subsidiary shrines. The middle part of the flight of steps was exposed in 1981 just outside the west wall of the Pump Room. The steps showed very considerable wear and had been cut back to take new treads, fragments of which still survived (fig. 22). An even earlier flight of steps could be seen in places beneath. That limestone steps could wear to this extent is a reflection of both the popularity of the building and the hobnail boots and sandals of the Romano-British population!

Of the flanking shrines very little is known, because the west wall of the Pump Room has obscured so much, but the position of the front of the north shrine has been located. The step upon which the superstructure was built was carefully examined and from the wear marks and discolorations due to weathering, still traceable on it, it was possible to show that the wall had been enlivened by corner pilasters and that the room was entered through a central door.

The rebuilding would have turned what was a purely classical temple into one far more like the native Romano-Celtic temples found all over north-western Europe. It is yet another fascinating example of the mixing of classical and native ideas, on what was

after all the extreme fringe of the Roman empire. The classical temple, put up, no doubt, under official patronage in the first century, was modified to suit local tastes and rituals a generation or two later by which time the local population had gained a new assurance under Roman rule and Romano–British architecture had come of age.

The sacrificial altar (figures 23–29)

About 15m in front of the temple stood the great sacrificial altar, at the point where the two principal visual axes of the temple com-

23 The stone base upon which the altar had once stood. The slabs are held together with clamps of iron set in lead. Discoloration and wear shows exactly where the altar stood and how much of the base was exposed.

24 The altar corner discovered in 1965 was carved on two adjacent sides with deities, one male, the other female. The naked male is the god Bacchus who holds a thyrsus and pours a drink to a panther squatting at his feet. The goddess cannot easily be identified, but the cornucopia which she holds beneath one arm and the libation flowing from the upturned vessel suggests that she is connected with fertility. Approx. 1.26m high.

plex crossed. All that survived in position was the raised platform of limestone slabs, still clamped together with ties of iron, upon which the altar had stood (fig. 23). The main platform measured 2.8m square and by tracing the worn and weathered areas around the edge, it was possible to show that the superstructure of the altar must have been 2.4m square.

By a remarkable series of chances we are able to reconstruct the altar in some detail. The first indication of what it would have looked like came in 1965 when, in the trial trench dug across the altar platform, one of the decorated altar corners was found, carved on two adjacent faces with deities (figs 9 and 24). One of the deities depicted is a naked male, probably Bacchus, shown holding a thyrsus in one hand and pouring a libation to a panther squatting at his feet.

25 Altar corner discovered in 1790. The clothed male figure is Jupiter, the naked male is the drinking Hercules – Hercules Bibax – who wears a lion-skin cloak, the paws knotted across his chest, and rests his left hand on a knobbed club. Approx. 1.26m high.

His companion, on the adjacent side, is a heavily draped female holding an upturned vase, from which liquid flows, merging with her drapery. In the crook of her right arm she supports what appears to be a cornucopia.

Within a few minutes of making the discovery a quick inspection of the Museum showed that a closely similar block had been found during the rebuilding of 1790 (fig, 25). Although badly weathered, it is possible to recognize the same paired deities, one naked, the other clothed. In this case the naked god was Hercules Bibax, the drinking Hercules, shown holding a large drinking vessel in one hand, the other resting on a knobbed club. Over his shoulders he wears a cape made of a lion's skin, the paws of which are knotted over his chest. The adjacent figure is Jupiter holding a trident in one

26 The third altar corner is built into a buttress at Compton Dando church 13km from Bath. The naked figure cannot be identified. The clothed figure is Apollo playing his lyre. Approx. 1.26m high.

hand while at his feet stands an eagle. Exactly where the stone was found is not recorded but, since the north wall of the 1790 Pump Room actually crosses the altar, it is not at all impossible that it was found there, within a metre or two of the 1965 discovery.

By an even more remarkable coincidence a third corner is known, built into the corner buttress of the church at Compton Dando, seven miles west of Bath (fig. 26). The block, now exposed to all weathers, is very badly eroded, but here again two adjacent figures can be traced, one naked, the other clothed. Unfortunately the naked figure is too weathered to allow identification, but his (or her) partner is shown with one foot on a rock, raised knee supporting a musical instrument and is therefore either Apollo or Orpheus. There can be very little doubt that all three blocks belong to the same monument: they are identical in size and base mouldings, and the pairing of the deities, one clothed, the other naked, is consistent. Moreover, stylistic similarities such as the body stance and the exceptionally thick necks provide a strong indication that all three were carved at least by the same school, if not by the same craftsman. How and why the Compton Dando block was dragged 13km from Bath we are unlikely to know, but it might be significant that both Compton Dando church and the central area of Bath, beneath which the altar lies, belonged to the same religious establishment. Perhaps cart-loads of old building stone, including the altar corner, were removed from the centre of Bath in the Middle Ages and used in adjacent church buildings. This is pure guesswork but it is at least possible.

We have, then, three of the four corner blocks of the altar, each with integral base mouldings but without the necessary capping mould. Fortunately, during the 1965 excavation, one of the moulded blocks which would have formed the working surface of the altar was discovered lying amid the rubble, close to the corner stone. Its cornice mouldings were simply carved in a style admirably suited to match the base, while its upper surface, which would have been exposed, was very carefully tooled to a smooth finish (figs 27 and 28) and slightly dished: this would have been a very distinct advantage during sacrifices, particularly when freshly slaughtered animals were being opened up for purposes of augury.

The 1965 trench, immediately in front of the altar, produced another remarkable discovery. Standing on the flagged floor of the temple precinct was an inscribed statue base (fig. 29) inscribed DEAE SVLI [To the Goddess Sulis] L.MARCIVS MEMOR [Lucius Marcius Memor] HARVSP [Haruspex] D.D. [gave this gift]. A *haruspex* was a high-ranking augurer whose job it was to foretell the future by examining the entrails of sacrifices made on the altar, or by interpreting the flight patterns of birds and other omens. It is interesting to know that the temple at Bath was of sufficient importance to attract a man of this status, who might normally be expected to practise only in the largest religious centres of the empire. It will be seen

54

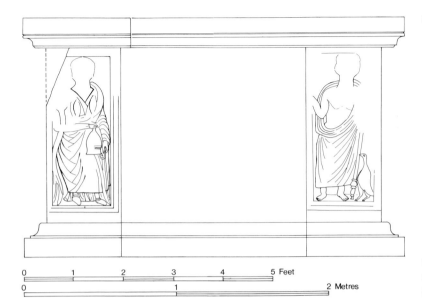

27 The altar reconstructed.

28 The altar corners replaced on their original base in the temple precinct.

from the illustration (fig. 29) that Memor's title had at first been abbreviated HAR, regularly laid out in relation to the other lettering, and only later was the VSP jammed in rather awkwardly at the end. It may be that *haruspices* were so rare in Britain that no one in Bath knew what HAR stood for and the temple authorities had to be more explicit.

The base had been placed on the latest paving level a little to the west of the altar: it is therefore not part of the original layout but was probably added late in the temple's life. The gift which Memor dedicated to the goddess was in all probability a statue erected immediately to the east of the inscription. Sadly nothing now survives of it except for a slot cut in the paving stones to take its base.

Again then, by a fortunate combination of chance discovery and planned excavation, it has been possible to reconstruct, almost

29 The trial excavation of 1965 exposed a dedicatory inscription still in its original position on the precinct floor. It records a gift, probably a statue, erected for the goddess Sulis Minerva by the temple augurer (*haruspex*) Lucius Marcius Memor. (Scale in feet.)

in its entirety, another of the town's major religious monuments. The great sacrificial altar emerges as a 1.5m-high mass of stone, with elaborately carved corners set on a raised platform in such a position that it would form the visual focus from all around. Memor's gift would have enhanced its dignity even more.

The enclosing colonnade

The temple, altar and the spring (to be described below), were enclosed in a single unified concept by a colonnaded verandah running along the north, west and south sides of the precinct. The east side was closed by a blank wall through which opened the main entrance. Most of the colonnade is now below parts of the town which cannot be excavated, but substantial sections of the north and west sides were seen by Irvine in 1867 and again by Wedlake in 1960. Part of the south side lay beneath the cellars of Stall Street, and in 1964 and 1968 trenches were dug to examine, at first hand, the details of its structure. As a result we now know that the outer wall was a blank enclosing wall serving to seal off the temple from the outside world, but 3m inside it was a ground-level stylobate (a foundation of large flat stone blocks), originally fronted by a stone gutter the position of which could still be traced. The stylobate would once have supported a colonnade which, in turn, would have taken a verandah roof sloping inwards so that the rain water would drain into the gutter. The overall result would have been to create a cloistered feeling, the verandah providing protection from rain and shade from the sun.

The temple occupied much of the western part of the precinct. Around it the precinct floor was simply gravel. The eastern part was differently treated. Strictly it was divided into three: a central paved area around the altar (the inner precinct), a southern part wholly occupied by the sacred spring, and a northern area about which little is known but which appears to have been simply surfaced with gravel. The paved area and the spring have been examined in considerable detail in the excavation programme of 1979 to 1983 and the entire structural history can now be worked out in fascinating detail.

THE TEMPLE AND ITS PRECINCT

The sacred spring and the inner precinct

The reason for the siting of the temple and the baths was the great spring which gushed out a third of a million gallons of mineral waters a day at a temperature of 42°C. Endowed, no doubt, with religious and curative properties by the pre-Roman inhabitants, it is not surprising that the Romans should have been so quick to exploit it.

The great volume of water must have created very serious difficulties for the Roman engineers and until the problems of its control were solved the central complex of public buildings could not be built. The first stage in the process of taming the waters would have been the creation of an efficient drainage system to remove excess water while building was in progress. Most of the great drain built at this time can still be followed and indeed it has been restored to its original Roman function of carrying off waste (fig. 30). It was built of rough stone walling of such proportions that a man could comfortably walk along it without stooping. In the bottom was a rectangular timber-lined gully to take the flow, with the timbers still preserved. At intervals along its length smaller subsidiary drains emptied in. Realizing that at such points and at changes in alignment there was the possibility of silting or of the clogging of inlets, the careful Roman engineers constructed rectangular manholes leading up to the street surface to provide those responsible for keeping the drains in good order with easy access. Once clear of the central area of the settlement, the drain appears to have emptied into an open leat which must originally have led to the River Avon. Now, however, the Roman drain flows into a complex network of mediaeval and later sewers before reaching the river.

As soon as the drain was in operation work could begin on the creation of a reservoir. The drain had conveniently lowered the water level at the spring head, enabling the engineers to get close to the vent. Next a ring-beam of close-spaced oak piles was rammed into the mud in a rough circle around all the outlets leaving a gap at the mouth of the drain. The piles served to consolidate the ground and provided a convenient working surface from which the mud

30 Details of the great drain which led excess water from the reservoir. The drain performs the same function today.

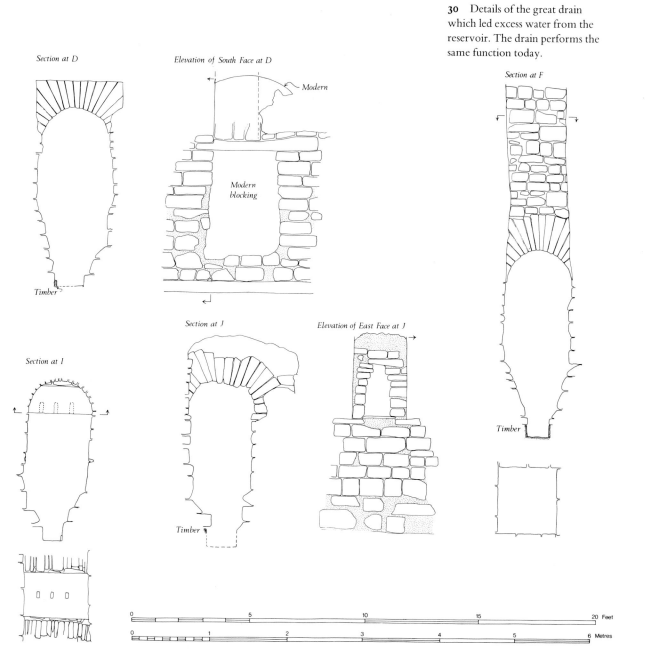

Section at D

Elevation of South Face at D

Modern

Modern blocking

Timber

Section at F

Section at I

Section at J

Elevation of East Face at J

Timber

Timber

Timber

0   5   10   15   20 Feet

0   1   2   3   4   5   6 Metres

and silt in the spring could be dug out. This done a foundation trench was then dug around the outside of the ring of piles and its bottom consolidated with piles to form a firm bedding for the reservoir wall. The wall was built of massive stone blocks, tightly fitted together without mortar, and rose to a maximum height of 2m above the inner pile ring. In its base, at the east side, a 30cm square vent was left for the water to escape into the drain and above the vent a sluice slot was created. Some idea of the work at this stage is given by fig. 31.

When the wall was complete the important process of water-proofing began. First, blue lias clay was puddled in around the tops of the wooden piles. Then the entire reservoir wall was lined inside with massive sheets of lead 1cm thick measuring some 2.4m by 1.8m and each weighing nearly half a ton. The upper edges were folded back across the wall while the lower edge was bent out and the lower angle sealed with a thick step of waterproof pink concrete with tiles set into the top. The vertical joins were made good by overlapping the sheets and burning the edges together (figs 32 and 33). The overall effect was to create a massive lead-lined container into which the water gushed through natural fissures in the base.

How the sluice slot was treated we do not know but it could simply and effectively have been sealed with baulks of timber. All this time the bottom vent was allowing the water to flow away. Finally, when the plumbing was complete, the vent was blocked with 30cm–square timber (which remained in position until Major Davis removed it in 1878!). Immediately the water would have risen until the reservoir was full and it was from the top that the hot water was channelled off to fill the Great Bath. At first sight it might seem rather unnecessary to go to such lengths simply to provide a constant flow for the bath, but the Roman engineers understood the waters well. They knew that the rapid flow brought up quantities of sand which would have clogged the plumbing in no time. By building the reservoir with its 2m head of water they ensured that the sediment would settle so that the water flowing from the top into the bath was clear. The sediment would, of course, have accumulated in the reservoir but it could be flushed out quite easily by opening the sluice, from time to time, allowing the head of water to wash the silt out through the main drain. It must have been with this problem in mind that the drain was constructed on a grand scale. Standing back from all the detail, there is no doubt that the engineers were highly skilled and were fully aware of the potential, and the difficulties, of the source. Their solution to the problem was as elegant as it was efficient.

We have been concerned so far with technical questions but we must not forget the context. The spring was a sacred location

31 Diagram showing an early stage in the construction of the reservoir. Excess water is carried away in the drain. The ring of piles consolidates the mud providing a convenient working platform. The reservoir wall of massive stone blocks is shown beginning to rise.

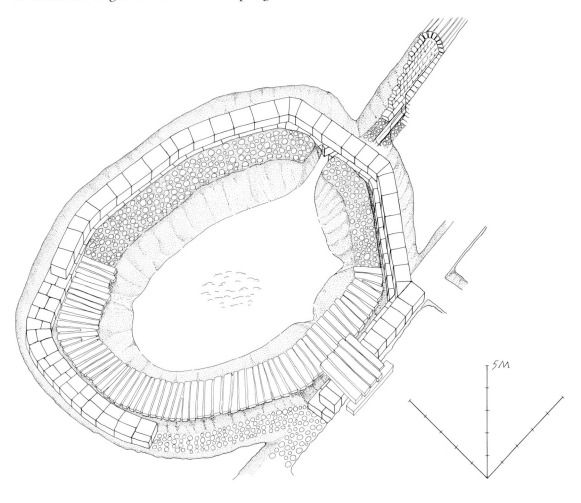

5M

32 Diagrammatic section through the reservoir wall and its foundations showing the way in which the waterproof lining of lead sheets was arranged.

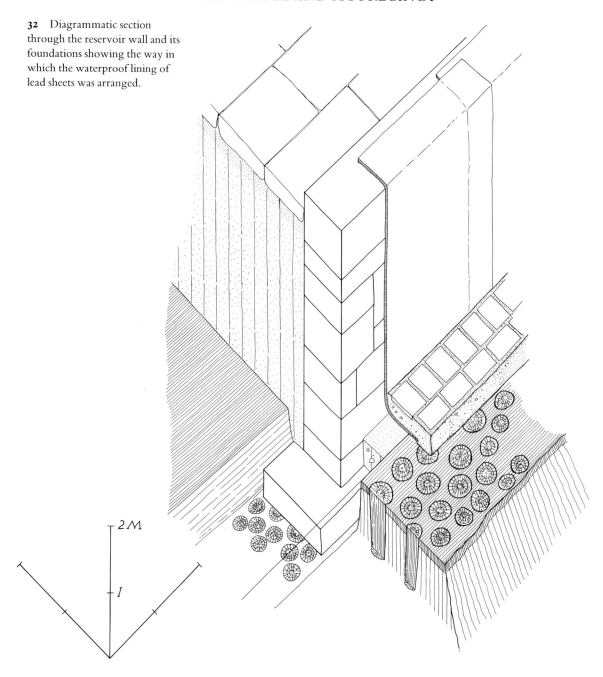

2M

1

and was enclosed within the temple precinct. It therefore had to be visually emotive as befits a place where the underworld of the gods was in communication with the everyday world. The simple elegance of the reservoir, full of hot bubbling water, deep green with a pall of vapour floating above the surface, cannot have failed to impress.

In the early stages the spring was open to the air, surrounded only by a low balustrade. On the south side was the hall of the bathing establishment penetrated by three large openings so that visitors could see the spring and come close to the sacred water, in exactly the same way as tourists do today (p. 112). To the north the entire area in front of the temple was paved on one level with massive slabs of limestone and in the centre was the altar. The eastern boundary

33 The reservoir during excavation. The wall blocks can be seen (left) stripped of their lead by Major Davis. The oak piles are still very well preserved. The massive pier was probably the base for a statue standing at what would have been the Roman water level.

at this stage was a plain wall perforated only by the main precinct entrance immediately opposite the altar. The emphasis of the entire layout was on simple uncluttered elegance.

The reservoir enclosure

Towards the end of the second century a dramatic, and indeed monumental, change was made to the temple precinct – the reservoir was enclosed within a massive rectangular chamber roofed with a tile and concrete vault. The thick walls of the enclosure, built of regular ashlar masonry with tile courses at intervals, still stand to a height of between 1 and 2m and can be seen along the north and east sides. The only means of access was a single narrow door set in the centre of the north wall directly south of the altar, presumably the way by which the officiating priest approached the spring. As part of this programme of renovation the height of the reservoir wall had been raised by about a metre. This meant that to give easy access from the precinct level three steps had to be provided up to the door sill, which was at the new level of the reservoir top.

Where the east wall crossed the outfall an arch was created above the capstone which covered the drain (fig. 34). In recent times water has been allowed to gush through the arch creating an impressive cascade, but it is difficult to see how this could have happened in the original arrangement since the Roman sluice slots are at too low a level. Moreover the courses of ashlar immediately above the capstone appear once to have continued across. The simplest explanation is that the arch was a relieving arch designed to take the weight of the wall off the capstone and that it was originally infilled with ashlar work. Massive steps down to the drain at this point have in the past been referred to as leading to a 'dipping place' where the water could be drunk. A more mundane (and more likely) suggestion is that they simply provided access to the drainage system to enable the sluice to be opened from time to time.

We have said that the reservoir enclosure was roofed. Dramatic evidence for this came from the excavation of the spring into which

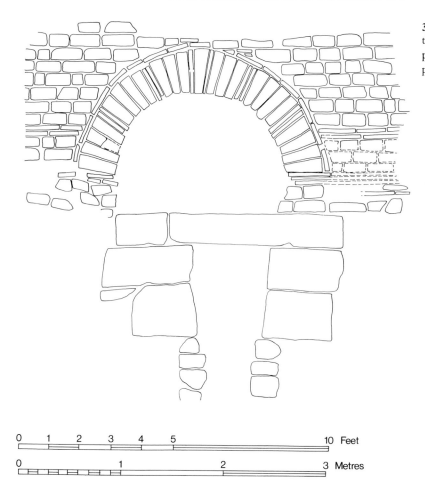

the great vault had collapsed (fig. 35). The excavation revealed most of its structural details – a spine of voussoir stones with brick ribs at intervals, the spaces between the ribs being filled with hollow box tiles to relieve the weight. So complete was the surviving detail that we can confidently offer a reconstruction (fig. 36). The only point of uncertainty is the nature of the openings in the lunettes: they must have existed to allow the steam to escape but no evidence of the detailed arrangement survives. Nor are we certain how the vault was finished but it was certainly coated with a layer of waterproof pink mortar and in all probability was left as a stark, unadorned concrete vault – a monument to technical competence: the Romans were never too worried about exteriors.

Interiors were another matter. The reservoir enclosure captured the spring in a watery gloom. Luxuriant ferns and mosses sprouting from the walls, birds swooping in and out, and the constant bubbling of the waters, would together have created the atmosphere of a vast natural grotto. It is difficult to believe that the enclosure was built for any reason other than to enhance the air of mystery, to impress the worshipper with the sanctity of the place. The effect was highlighted in another way. Seven massive bases were built up from the reservoir bottom to the surface of the water. Three were circular and four were square: all were only roughly dressed but since they

35 The vault which once roofed the reservoir enclosure collapsed and fell into the spring. The spine of the vault and its brick ribs can clearly be seen (cf. fig. 36).

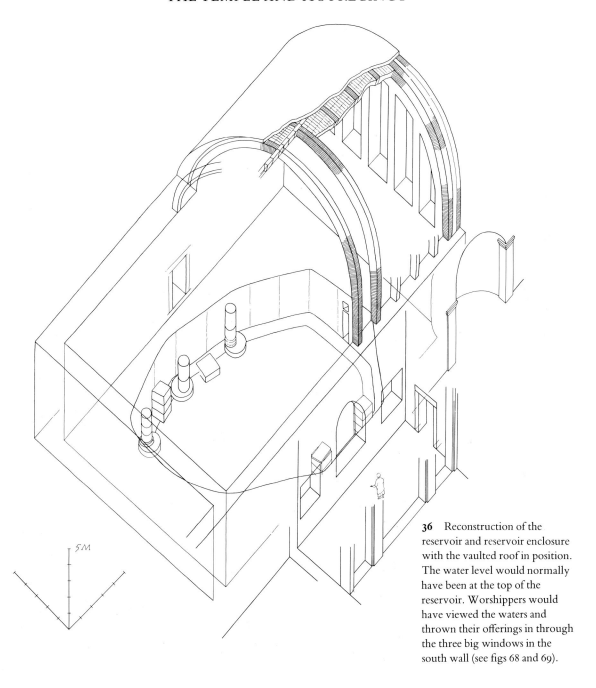

36 Reconstruction of the reservoir and reservoir enclosure with the vaulted roof in position. The water level would normally have been at the top of the reservoir. Worshippers would have viewed the waters and thrown their offerings in through the three big windows in the south wall (see figs 68 and 69).

5M

would have been entirely beneath the water this would not have mattered. Of their purpose we can only speculate, the most satisfying suggestion being that the bases supported statues – perhaps of water nymphs and gods – or a combination of statues and columns. On a cold winter morning, when white steam was swirling above the water, the effect of the floating figures in the limpid half light would have been electrifying.

At a more practical level, the construction of the reservoir necessitated other changes. Since a considerable volume of water would pour off the vault into the precinct, a ground level gutter had to be set in the paving outside the north wall of the reservoir to drain water away to the main outfall. There were also some changes made to the eastern boundary wall involving a considerable thickening particularly of the gate which may have been monumentalized at this stage. Finally, it was quite probably at this period that the temple was extended in the manner described above (pp. 48–50). Together these rebuildings would have changed the original temple complex out of all recognition.

The inner precinct in the third and fourth centuries

The great reservoir enclosure was a construction of no small technical skill. The flanks of the vault must have exerted a considerable thrust on the north and south walls but this was anticipated. The south wall already existed: it was thin but the buttressing effect of the side walls of the hall to the south meant that no additional thickening was needed. The new north wall, however, was built twice the thickness and no doubt had massive foundations in addition. Even so this was not enough.

Gradual subsidence or settling must have occurred. There would probably have been signs of cracking and then the north east corner seems to have sheared away. Immediate remedial action had to be taken, but the problem was how to provide strengthening buttressing along the north wall without making the structure unsightly and impinging too much upon the precinct.

The solution adopted was both inspired and effective. Quite simply a raised portico was created along the entire north wall incorporating three buttresses. At both the north-east and north-west corners these buttresses were massively built of large stone blocks clamped together with iron ties. The north-west buttress seems to have been in the form of an arch, but since it was taken down and replaced later the details are obscure. The north east buttress was quite solid but with a recess in the west face echoing the width of the western arch. The central buttress was disguised as a quadrifrons (a two-way arch with four supports) the whole serving as a monumental porch to the door leading to the spring. How the rest of the structure was treated is less clear though there were probably additional piers along the new façade supporting an entablature, and quite possibly the portico behind was vaulted. The overall effect of these additions

37 The temple precinct after excavation looking east across the altar towards the entrance. The raised portico (right) was built in front of the reservoir enclosure, part of the wall of which can be seen with its small central door leading to the spring.

was to create a solid buttressing mass along the entire length of the north wall giving the appearance of a grandiose façade.

The centre-piece of this new arrangement was the monumental porch of which the lower parts of the front piers remain in position (fig. 37) and blocks of the upper part have been found lying in the rubble collapse. From these it is possible to give some idea of the superstructure. It seems that the main doorway was an arched opening flanked by pilasters which would have supported an entablature. Unusually for north-western Europe, the arch was set in a triangular pediment which was elaborately sculpted. Although only a few of the original blocks survive they are sufficient to show the general arrangement – a central rock from which water is gushing flanked by two lightly clothed water nymphs holding a roundel above the rock in which was probably depicted the head of the god Sol – the god of the sun (figs 38–40). The symbolism is quite clear – Sol presiding over the waters – a highly appropriate design for such a position,

38 Reconstruction of the pediment of the monumental doorway in the centre of the portico. Water nymphs on either side of a rock from which water flows hold up a roundel very probably containing the head of the sun god Sol.

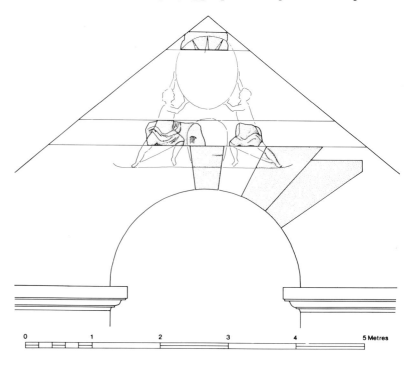

70

39 One of the blocks from the pediment showing a nymph and the flowing water (cf. fig. 38).

40 Voussoir block from the pediment with the foot of a nymph (cf. fig. 38).

only a few metres from the narrow door giving access to the spring! It raises the very interesting question of whether Sulis was also a sun god in Celtic mythology. If so the conflation of the male Sulis with the female Minerva would be most unusual but in the Celtic fringes this amusing play of opposites may well have been acceptable – it was very much in the Celtic spirit and we shall meet it again in a moment.

Now, it will be evident from the plan that the new portico impinged quite considerably upon the inner precinct and would have created an unacceptable asymmetry, unless, that is, an equivalent

71

41 Reconstruction of the temple and inner precinct in its most evolved state in the fourth century A.D.

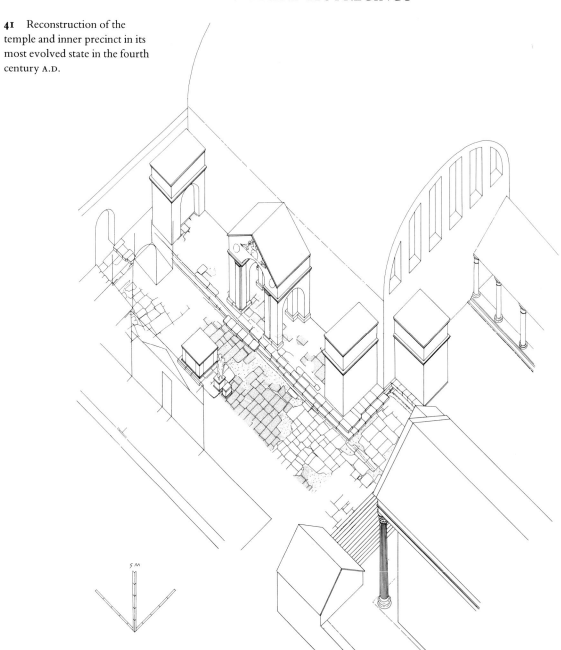

façade of some kind was erected to the north of the altar to maintain a visual balance. Unfortunately, this area is now entirely obscured by the north wall of the Pump Room and we will never know for certain what was done, but from the mass of tumbled stone recovered from the general area at various times during the last 300 years comes part of a monumental façade known as the Façade of the Four Seasons (for details see below pp. 84–8) which may well have occupied this position. The idea is even more attractive when we note that the Façade probably incorporated a pediment with the head of the moon goddess, Luna, in the centre (figs 56 and 57). It would have been a most satisfying balance to have had the moon goddess, Luna, facing the sun god, Sol, across the altar: again the tension of paired opposites!

The buttressing of the reservoir wall necessitated the removal of part of the eastern wall of the precinct which was rebuilt further to the east with a colonnaded walk on the outside. The original monumental eastern door was retained and was joined to the new doorway by a stylobate which may well have taken a screen wall of some kind to obscure a rather unsightly backwater in the south-eastern corner of the reconstructed precinct. The retention of the old doorway is interesting: it was structurally unnecessary, and indeed inconvenient, but since it marked the original entrance to the precinct it must have had symbolic significance as a boundary marker and thus had to be kept even though it would have been far simpler to have demolished it altogether.

The construction of the portico marked a major stage in the history of the temple and saw the monument at its most elaborate. Thereafter what changes there were were comparatively minor (fig. 41).

It seems that there were still problems with the stability of the north-west corner of the reservoir enclosure. Eventually the arched buttress was pulled down and a new solid buttress, echoing that at the east end of the portico, was put up together with a new buttress against the west wall. The alterations disturbed the regularity of the portico façade, all of which, except for the quadrifrons, was pulled

42 Gold earring with inset carbuncle from the spring. Overall length 3.7cm.

down. It was as part of this programme of alterations that the steps of the portico were renewed and the portico, together with the area around the altar, was repaved with slabs of blue pennant sandstone. Later alterations were much less significant and gradually the old precinct began to take on a shabby, patched appearance, before decay finally set in (pp. 209–13).

The spring and the worshippers

The spring held a considerable power over visitors to the temple because it was here that they could come closest to the divinities of the underworld and in particular to Sulis Minerva who presided over the waters. The simplest way to communicate with the goddess was to throw messages and offerings into the water, and this was done with great enthusiasm throughout the four hundred years of the temple's life. Heavy objects thrown in would sink to the bottom of the reservoir and into the quicksand below, where the constant turbulence of the spring would churn them up all together. Lighter objects would float or lie in the surface of the sand only to be washed into

43 Six of the thirty-three gem stones found in the culvert flowing from the spring. The collection probably represents a bag of gems thrown into the water by a worshipper. (Scale approx. $\frac{2}{1}$)

the drain when the sluice was opened. When Richard Mann opened up the drain in 1878 many valuable items were found. A gold earring with an inset carbuncle (fig. 42), a pin with a pearl attached, and a bag containing 33 exquisitely engraved gem stones (fig. 43) – all were presumably thrown into the spring and were washed into the culvert. One of the most dramatic objects to be found at this time was a ceremonial tin mask (fig. 44), quite probably a ritual object

44 Larger than life-size mask of tin which had once been attached to a wooden backing. The wood prevented the mask from sinking to the bottom of the reservoir and caused it to float out into the culvert where it was found 1,500 years later. Presumably it would originally have served in one of the temple rituals. (Height 33cm.)

belonging to the temple. It may once have been attached to a backing of wood therefore making it light enough to float.

The heavier objects sank into the silts of the spring and there remained, the collapsed vaulted roof eventually sealing them in. When Major Davis cleared the spring he left most of the fallen vault in position, but around the edges, where the silt was higher, resting on the tile surround, he was able to excavate part of the ritual deposit producing large numbers of coins, several pewter vessels (figs 45 and

45 and 46 Jug and candlestick of pewter. Votive offering, found by Major Davis in 1878 in the reservoir or in the culvert. Jug 19.4cm high; candlestick 24.4cm high.

46) and a curse inscribed on a sheet of pewter. This was a foretaste of things to come for in 1979 and 1980 we were able to remove the collapsed vault and dig deeper into the ritual deposit filling the spring.

What emerged was a remarkable display of offerings: between ten and twenty thousand coins, many silver and four gold; handled cups and other metal vessels of pewter, silver and bronze inscribed with dedications to the goddess Sulis Minerva; a large collection of some ninety pewter curses; a magnificent inlaid penannular brooch (fig. 53) and a range of other items including the head of a ritual silver rattle, floral bronze decorations possibly from the priests' robes (fig. 52), an amulet of breasts carved from elephant ivory (fig. 50) and, rather incongruously, a bronze washer from a model of a ballista (a kind of large-scale spring gun) (fig. 51).

The vast quantity of coinage gives some idea of how powerful the goddess was in the minds of the worshippers. Although much of it was low value bronze and brass there was a number of silver denarii, worth a day's pay for a working man, and four gold coins each of which would have meant two months' salary for a fairly high-ranking official – altogether a rather different level of response from the 2p and 10p pieces which today's visitors throw into the circular bath!

The metal vessels, jugs, handled cups, plates and bowls are particularly interesting (fig. 47). Many of them are inscribed to the goddess and it is quite possible that at least some of the pieces were the temple plate, discarded in this way when worn out or replaced. The prevalence of handled cups raises the question of whether the waters were drunk, but this seems unlikely and in all probability the vessels were used for pouring libations.

But it is the curses that bring us closest to the people. To inspire the goddess to work on your behalf it would have been necessary to write a message, in correct official language, on a sheet of pewter and to consign it to the waters, either flat or rolled up (figs 48 and 49). A typical curse would ask the goddess to bring down some terrible vengeance on someone who had done you wrong and there would follow a list of suspects among whom the goddess would know which one to punish. The curse found by Major Davis is a good example of this; it begins: 'May he who carried off Vilbia from me become as liquid as the water. May she who so obscenely devoured her become dumb' and then follows a list of eight suspects. This, at any rate, was the traditional reading but there is now some doubt as to its accuracy and the suggestion has been made that what was carried off was not a girl but a bath towel, rather spoiling the possibilities of turning the curse into a good story!

Another of the same kind found in 1979 reads: 'To the Goddess Sulis Minerva [from] Docca. I give to your divinity the money which

47 Two pewter and one silver paterae found together with others in the sacred spring in 1979–80. All were inscribed with dedications to the goddess Sulis Minerva.

48 One of the pewter curses here unrolled. It records the petition of Roveta and lists the names of ten people, several of them slaves, among them the malefactor who Roveta was cursing. Max. height 7.0cm.

49 Four of the curses which had been rolled up before being thrown into the spring. Height of longest 5.0cm.

I have lost [by theft], that is five denarii; and may he who [has stolen it] whether slave [or free, whether man or woman] is to be compelled . . .' and here the curse breaks off. Another is even more interesting: 'Whether pagan or Christian, whosoever, whether man or woman, whether boy or girl, whether slave or free, has stolen from me, Annianus, in the morning six silver pieces from my purse, you, lady Goddess, are to extract [them] from him. If through some deceit he has given me [. . .], and do not give thus to him, but [. . .] his blood who has invoked this on me.' The second side of the sheet lists eighteen suspects. Here, the aggrieved Annianus is hedging his bets in all directions. The first part is all-embracing enough to make sure no one was excluded. The second part, though rather obscure, seems to be an attempt to make any counter spell which the thief had set in motion rebound on him. The inclusion of the word 'Christian' clearly implies that in the fourth century Christianity had firmly established itself even in such an ancient pagan town as Bath.

It is tempting to wonder whether Annianus was not also responsible for a second curse which simply reads: 'I have given to the goddess, Sulis, the six silver pieces which I have lost. It is for the goddess to extract it from the debtors written below.' Three names are listed among whom one, Senicianus, also occurs on the first curse. Could it be that having failed with this one, Annianus had another written with a longer list of suspects and more all-embracing wording? While it is possible, the recurrence of the name and the similarity of the sum may be nothing more than coincidence.

It is clear from two of those quoted that a kind of official language was being used 'whether it be X or Y', rather like the all-inclusive language of solicitors today. Without the correct wording a curse would fail or misfire. No doubt one had to pay (then as now) to have an expert write the draft. In this respect it is particularly interesting that the last curse mentioned ended with the statement 'The draft has been copied'. What exactly this means is not clear but it could be that the scribe wrote a draft which the person placing the curse then copied out on a pewter sheet with his own hand. This could explain the variety of handwritings.

So far we have considered only the curses dealing with people who stole things. Money, a bath towel, a bracelet and a hooded cloak are all mentioned – but another use of the divine power was adjudicating in disputes. This is illustrated by one third-century text which mentions a family group – Uricalus, his wife and two children and his brother Decentinus and his wife. All are listed as 'The names of those who have sworn at the spring to the Goddess Sulis on the twelfth of April. Whosoever there has perjured himself you are to make him pay for it to the goddess Sulis in his own blood.' Clearly there was a family dispute in which one person was lying – the goddess would know who it was and would exact punishment.

Together these texts provide a fascinating insight into provincial life in all its pettiness, what it was that made people irate and how they relied heavily on the presiding deity to help them at every turn. For a miscreant, even if undetected, to suspect that he had been named and cursed must have been a fearsome uncertainty to live with.

Minerva, and thus presumably Sulis Minerva, had many attributes – she was a goddess of wisdom and of healing and she also possessed martial characteristics. One might expect, therefore, some indication of all this at the sacred spring. At some healing springs it was quite usual for the sick and lame to dedicate to the deity a model, usually in wood, of whatever part of their anatomy was diseased. Deposits of arms, legs, eyes and other parts have been found in France at the shrine of Sequanna at the source of the Seine and at the spring of Chamalières not far from Vichy. Bath is devoid of offerings of this type except for the single piece of ivory carved stylistically in the form of breasts (fig. 50). If, however, wooden *ex votos* had been thrown in they would have floated away when the sluice was open. It is sad that nothing of this kind has survived.

Of the deity's war-like attributes we have some hints. The washer from a model ballista (fig. 51) could well have been an offering made by a soldier as thanks for some service the goddess had rendered, or in anticipation of help. That Bath was evidently popular among the army is shown by the number of military tombstones in the vicinity put up long after the garrison had moved on. Perhaps

50 Ivory votive offering, probably symbolic of female breasts. From the spring. 7.0cm across.

51 Bronze washer from a catapult (ballista) from the spring. Diameter 8cm.

52 Fine bronze sheet decoration probably once attached to cloth, perhaps the priest's robes. Found in the spring. Max. width 18cm.

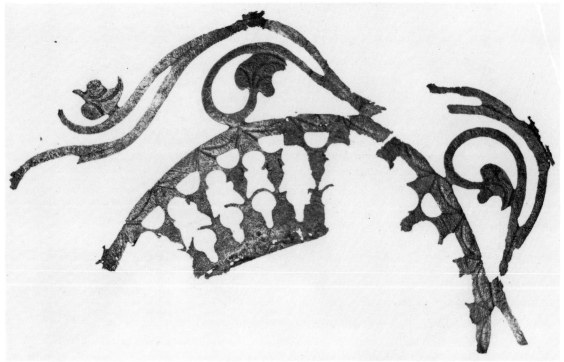

they were of soldiers who had returned to the city in their retirement to settle, or of the wounded making a pilgrimage in anticipation of a cure. We will see what kind of men they were later (Chapter 7). They would have been among the tens of thousands of people who at one time or another crowded around the three large windows in the south wall of the enclosure to see the waters, to be close to the deity and to seek her help.

53 Penannular brooch of bronze with terminals inset with red enamel (see enlargement). The scenes may reflect a story from Celtic mythology. Found in the spring. Max. diameter 6.8cm.

54 Some of the sculptured stones found in 1790 and later belonged to a substantial monument divided into panels by fluted pilasters. Between each pair of pilasters were two niches, the lower with a shell canopy protecting a life-size seated figure, the upper depicting a cupid representing a season: Spring holds a bunch of flowers, Summer a corn ear, Autumn fruit and Winter a bill-hook for chopping firewood. (For scales see fig. 55.)

The Façade of the Four Seasons

So far we have been concerned with buildings and structures whose actual sites are known. The excavations have, however, produced large quantities of building stone and sculptured blocks from other monuments sited somewhere within the precinct, otherwise unknown apart from their constituent parts. Of these, the most remarkable is the Façade of the Four Seasons, of which fourteen pieces were found in 1790, one in 1895, another in 1968 and two more scraps in 1982. Many attempts have been made at reconstruction,

but only recently have all the pieces been satisfactorily fitted into place in relation to one another (figs 54 and 55).

The façade was provided with six fluted pilasters belonging to a simplified Tuscan order, dividing the wall into five spaces 1.2m wide, the central space serving as a doorway. The other four were treated in similar ways, each being provided with a large niche roofed with a shell canopy protecting a seated figure, above which was a small recess containing a running cupid. The cupids are particularly well represented among the surviving fragments: one holding a

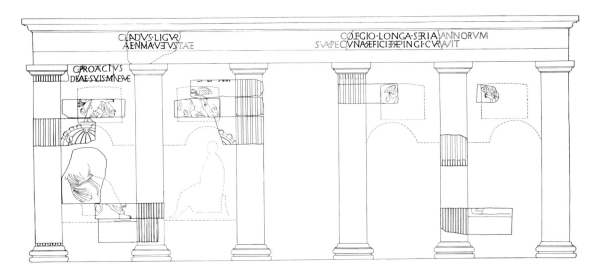

55 Reconstruction of the Façade of the Four Seasons.

bunch of flowers is evidently playing the part of Spring, Summer is carrying corn, Autumn holds a bunch of fruit, while Winter brandishes a billhook for cutting firewood. Of the large seated figures below, only scraps survive, but one at least, the figure below the cupid Spring, is a heavily draped female who appears to be holding a large bud over one shoulder. It seems likely that she, too, is Spring, in which case the cupids are acting out the roles of the figures below.

Immediately above the cupid recesses ran a two-line inscription, of which the section above Spring is complete. It reads, *C. Protacius . . . deae Sulis Minervae*, 'Gaius Protacius . . . of the goddess Sulis Minerva' – a clear reminder that the façade is closely connected with the presiding deity. Presumably the inscription was meant to be read one line at a time right across the façade. Another two-line inscription was carved on the frieze above the pilasters. Only fragments survive, but they may be translated as 'Claudius Ligur . . . excessive age . . . the guild in a long sequence of years . . . at its own cost had it repaired and repainted . . .'. A tantalizing fragment, but sufficient to show that a building which had suffered from excessive age was repaired and repainted by a guild of craftsmen with which one Claudius Ligur

86

was in some way associated. The building must be one of the temple structures, as the words *deae Sulis Minervae* imply; whether it was the temple itself or the structure to which the façade belonged will never be known.

The excavations of 1790 also produced three carved blocks belonging to a pediment 5.5m long and 1.5m high, carved in the centre with a roundel containing the head of the goddess Luna, shown here heavily draped with her hair piled in a high bun on the top of her head (fig. 56). In her hand she carries a riding whip, whilst behind the head, shallowly carved, is a crescent moon. The corners of the pediment appear to be enlivened with globes, but of these little survives. The style of the carving is in many ways very similar to that of the Façade of the Four Seasons, hinting that the two may belong together. In fact, when the measurements are compared, it will be seen that the pediment fits precisely over the central doorway

56   Above the Façade of the Four Seasons there was probably a pediment. It may well be that the four pediment blocks found in 1790 belong to it. Together they show the goddess Luna with a crescent moon behind her head and a riding whip in one hand.

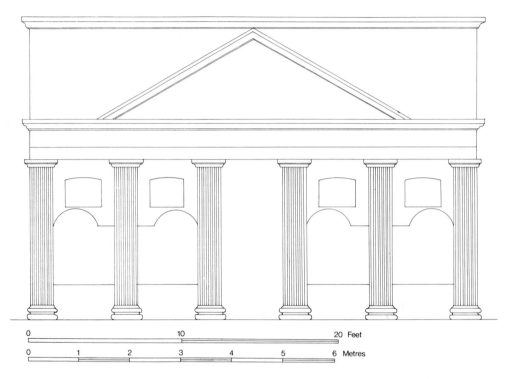

57 Suggested reconstruction of the façade and pediment.

58 A lively young hound squatting at the feet of someone most likely to be the goddess Diana, whose bow can be seen above the hound's body. Found in the temple precinct re-used as paving in 1982. Max. height 75cm.

and the two adjacent interpilaster spaces (fig. 57); clearly the two elements are designed to fit the same rules of proportion and it may well be that the reconstruction offered here approximates closely to the truth. There are, of course, alternatives: for example, the façade might have belonged to a side wall whilst the pediment formed part of the end wall of the same building, but until the actual foundations are located within the precinct we are unlikely ever to know.

The exact location of the monument may well never be fixed but the position in which the fallen blocks were found shows that it must have been somewhere in the vicinity of the inner precinct. The recent excavations have now removed a number of the possibilities leaving the site north of the altar as the most reasonable guess. As we have seen (p. 73), in such a location it would have neatly balanced the main portico attached to the north side of the reservoir to the south of the altar. Here the problem rests.

88

THE TEMPLE AND ITS PRECINCT

Diana's hound (figure 58)

One of the prize discoveries of the 1981–3 excavation was a fragment of a relief (in two parts) depicting a playful young hound squatting at the feet of a draped figure and looking up at her. Part of a bow, carved just above the animal's back, leaves little doubt that we are dealing with a relief of the hunting goddess Diana. The skill of the sculptor in presenting the tensed energy of the beast is quite exceptional. It is reminiscent of several other fine animal carvings from

59 Reconstruction of the niched quadrangular monument two blocks of which were found re-used as paving in the temple precinct.

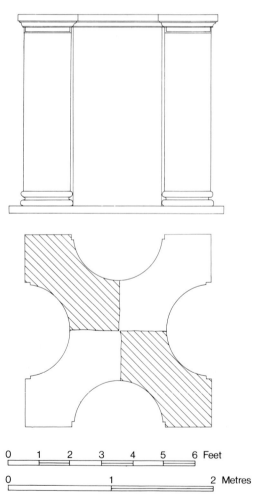

0 1 2 3 4 5 6 Feet

0   1   2 Metres

90

the Bath region which may have come from the same hand or school. The nature of the monument and its location are beyond recovery: the surviving fragments were reused in a later reflooring.

The large free-standing monument (figure 59)

Davis's excavation of 1895 produced two flat blocks which had been used at a late date as paving slabs or steps but had originally formed part of the cornice of an elaborately carved monument about 2m square and standing to a height of 2.4–2.8m. Each of the four sides was cut to form a deep recess protecting a standing, life-size figure, but all that now remains in the top of one of the recesses is the crest of a helmet and the tip of a spear belonging to a single military personage. The external corners of the monument were simply carved to give the appearance of flanking pilasters supporting a highly decorated cornice. The quality of the work is extremely fine, but where originally the structure stood we are unlikely ever to know. It must represent one of the many monuments pulled down in the sub-Roman period and used as paving.

Dedicatory altars (figure 120)

The temple precinct was provided with a number of lesser monuments, such as dedicatory inscriptions and small altars, which were probably tucked away in corners or against walls. Two of these, found in 1790, were both erected to the deity Sulis for a retired centurion, Marcus Aufidius Maximus, by slaves whom he appears to have set free (p. 185). Other inscriptions were put up to the goddess by Priscus, a stone mason of the Carnutes, near Chartres, and by Quintus Pompeius Aniecetus. These can have formed only a few of large numbers of similar inscriptions which must have cluttered the precinct. When it is remembered that all of the monuments described above stood somewhere in the eastern half of the precinct in front of the temple, and that by the very nature of the excavations large quantities of sculptures must still remain to be found, some idea of

(a)

(b)

(c)

the ornate and densely packed atmosphere of the temple emerges. Somehow the temple authorities would have jammed in these expressions of piety, still leaving room for ritual and worship. Walking through the aisles of the abbey, only a few metres away, and looking at the closely packed dedications, it is possible to recapture something of the self-expression and parade common to both Roman and Christian religion.

60 Deities from Roman Bath: (a) Minerva, found in the Great Bath (69 cm high); (b) Loucetius, the horned god and Nemetona with three hooded figures and an animal, found in the Great Bath (43 cm high); (c) A triad of mother goddesses found at Cleveland Walk. The carving, though simple and crude, is a dramatic example of native art. Height 24 cm high.

4

DISCOVERY OF THE BATHS

The construction of the famous Stall Street sewer of 1727, which produced the first indication of the temple – the head of Minerva – also led to the discovery of the baths, for in July 1727, at a depth of 4.9m below the street, the workmen hacked through a floor made of hollow box-tiles mortared together side by side and covered with a course of flat tiles. An annotated sketch of the trench produced by a Belgian, Bernard Lens, on 20 August, leaves little doubt that the discovery was part of a hypocaust, now known to belong to the south-west corner of the bathing establishment, the hollow box-tiles allowing hot air to circulate freely beneath the floor of the room. Indeed the contemporary notes record 'black stuff very like soot' inside the tiles.

The next discovery was altogether more spectacular. In 1755 work began on the construction of a suite of baths, called the Duke of Kingston's Baths, over the site of the west range of the abbey claustral buildings, at this date known as the Abbot's House. The softness of the ground hereabouts demanded deep footings, and it is hardly surprising that immediately the soil removal began, archaeological details started to emerge: first the remains of a Saxon

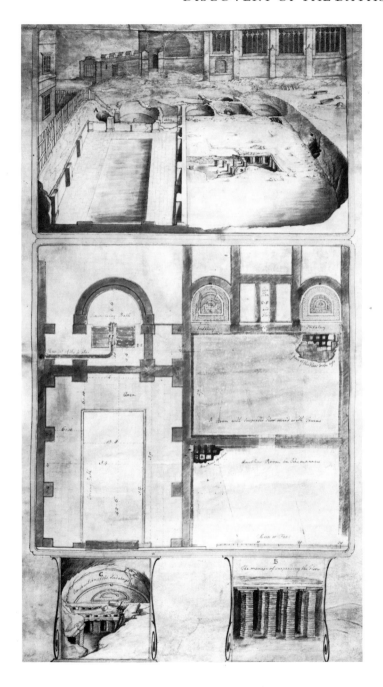

61 The first major discovery of the baths came in 1755 when the Duke of Kingston's Baths were being constructed. Much of the east end of the Roman bathing establishment was exposed. Fortunately several competent antiquaries were present at the time to record discoveries. The illustration here is of a drawing of 1755 now in the British Museum (No. Add. 21577 Bi).

cemetery and later most of what is now known to be the east end of the Roman bathing establishment, excellently preserved. Such a staggering discovery naturally attracted widespread interest. The work was closely watched and recorded by Dr Charles Lucas with the help of John Wood, the architect, and an account was published in his *Essays on the Waters* in 1756; but perhaps the most evocative description was provided by the artist William Hoare, then resident in Bath. In 1762 he sent a plan and perspective of excavations, together with a covering letter to a now unknown member of the aristocracy (fig. 61). His illustration and letter speak for themselves:

Bath. July 24.1762.

My Lord,

With this I have sent your Lordship a copy of my Plan and View of the Roman Baths in the state they appeared when first discovered, to which is added part of the South side of the Abbey to shew their Situation.

In the Perspective View your Lordship will see in a Room adorned with Corinthian Pillasters an Oblong Bath with its Area and Descent by Steps, and contiguous to it a smaller semicircular Bath with a descent of six very high steps, as appears by the Plan, but extremely wore by the Foot. In the shaded part at A is the Spring and Channel of the water.

The other large Room has two Ludatories belonging to it, with tessellated Pavements, which are exactly drawn in the Plan. in the middle between these is the Fireplace and Flue for heating the Rooms. The Floor is suspended on Pillars of square Brick, as in the drawing beneath the Plan at B.

C shews the manner of the Ludatorys, with their tubulated Bricks, which were continued up and along all the walls of the Room.

Near one of the Ludatories the Floor is broke up to show its construction.

On the Brick Pillars which are 9 inches square and four feet high lies a Flagstone Cap one inch and half high, and sixteen

inches square, over which are placed bricks two feet square and
two inches thick, and the whole is covered with Terras.

I am with great Respect

Your Lordships most obliged

humble servant

William Hoare.

My daughter desires to join with me her most dutiful Respects
to Your Lordship and the Ladies.

Important though the remains were, antiquarian amusements were
strictly subservient to hard cash and by 1763 the new baths had completely replaced the old. Subsidiary works carried out in the same
year immediately to the south added a few more details, but there
the matter rested.

The discoveries of 1727 and 1755 had more or less defined the
west and east limits of the establishments, while drainage works in
Abbey Passage and Union Street between 1799 and 1803 sectioned
exedrae belonging to the north and south sides. Thus, by the beginning of the nineteenth century it could be said that the baths occupied
an area approximately 40m by 90m. Limited alterations to the engine
room in the south-west corner of the site, close to the 1727 finds,
uncovered part of a hypocaust in 1825 but the discoveries were not
followed up at the time.

It is fair to say that renewed interest in the bathing establishment
was entirely due to James Irvine. Previously, when finds had been
accidentally made, they were recorded and filled in again, with no
further attempts at research. Irvine's presence in Bath altered all this.
He was essentially a man of insatiable curiosity who, having collected
information about previous discoveries, was not satisfied to let the
matter rest. He wanted to know more and the only way to ac-
complish this was by excavation. In September 1867 he obtained permission to explore the cellars immediately south of the Duke of
Kingston's Bath, and in odd moments during the following months
he carried out a trial excavation, exposing a semicircular bath, doors
and adjacent walls. This was the first purely research excavation to

be undertaken in the city. All the time he was keeping watch on the building work on the temple site. In December 1869 the old engine room in the south-west corner of the site was undergoing alterations at the hand of the City Engineer, Major Davis. Irvine, needless to say, was present and busily recorded everything exposed – including a substantial part of a *tepidarium*, a latrine and a number of other details. He was not content with plans and verbal descriptions, but drew fine archaeological sections through the deposits

62 Plan to show how little of the bathing establishment was known as late as 1870.

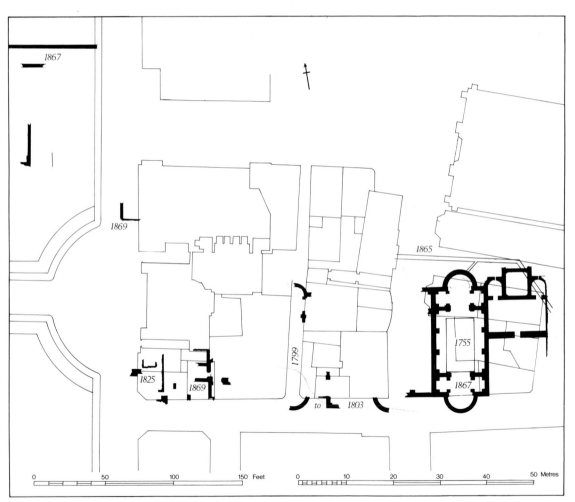

which choked the building after its abandonment, providing the only sections relevant to the end of the baths ever to be recorded (fig. 62).

The next major step forward came in 1871, when Major Davis had his men dig a trench in Abbey Passage to explore the possibility of blocking a leak in the King's Bath. About 6m down they exposed Roman masonry, now known to be close to the north-west corner of the Great Bath. Using extremely powerful pumps to keep the water-level down, he first explored an area of the ambulatory paving and then exposed the massive steps leading down to the Great Bath. At the bottom he came upon the sheet lead lining the bath floor and, unable to resist the temptation, cut a 30cms square out of it to examine the footings beneath. The hole can still be seen when the bath is emptied. At this stage, however, the proprietors of the Kingston Baths began to complain that the pumps had so lowered the water-table that their own bath could no longer be filled. Rather than face legal action, further work was suspended and the trench vaulted over. But seven years later, after the Kingston Baths had been acquired by the city, Davis returned to the problem of the leak – a problem which eventually led him, as we have already seen (p. 22), to the excavation of the main Roman drain and the sacred spring.

The discoveries of 1878–9 caused a great deal of excitement locally and in an atmosphere of Victorian beneficence a fund was opened, under the sponsorship of the City Council, to buy up the superincumbent properties so that excavation could proceed unhindered. Gradually, throughout 1880–1, those parts of the Great Bath now in public ownership were uncovered, the earth and rubble being removed by a horse and cart trudging up a ramp of earth leading to York Street (figs 63–65). No attempt was made to record the stratigraphy. The great vaulted roof which had fallen into the bath was shovelled away without any note being taken, only the larger pieces being left in position, and architectural details were stacked on one side with hardly a mention of their original positions being recorded. Even by the archaeological standards of the time, the activity was little short of disastrous. This was chiefly because there was no one of Irvine's curiosity and calibre associated with the work. Richard

63 The main phase of excavation at the baths took place during the 1880s under the direction of Major Davis. The buildings above were bought up and demolished. The photograph shows the sixteenth-century Queen's Bath in the process of destruction. Beneath it was found the Roman Circular Bath.

Mann, the builder employed by Davis, did his best, but relations between the two men were fast deteriorating, leaving Mann without the time or the facilities to record in the detail he would have wished.

But worse was to come as the excavations moved west. The sixteenth century Queen's Bath was totally destroyed and from 1883–5 the Roman Circular Bath and the adjacent corridors were exposed, and then from 1885–7 the complex of heated baths which constitute the west range was cleared, in what can only be described as a desultory way, immediately to be covered up again by the douche

100

and massage baths, totally obscuring large areas of Roman work before adequate records could be made. There was uproar in the archaeological world. In July 1886, J. Henry Middleton, the local secretary for Gloucester of the Society of Antiquaries, was 'directed by the Council' to inspect 'the work now being done under the supervision of Mr. Davis, the City Architect at the newly discovered portion of the Roman Baths at Bath'. He reported that:

New walls and pilasters carrying arches are now being built on this Roman work; and the whole will be roofed in. This is much to be regretted. The remains would, of course, have been far more interesting and instructive if the whole had been roofed in with some light iron structure supported on iron columns, arranged

64 The Great Bath c. 1886, still cluttered with sculptured stones found during the excavation suffering from exposure to the weather.

in such a way as to span the whole place without raising any new structure on the ancient walls; but this method would probably have been more troublesome than the present scheme of 'restoration' which is being carried out. The present somewhat objectional scheme is, however, being carried out (so far) with care, and with as little damage as possible to the Roman remains. There appears to have been some suggestion that the circular bath should be again used for baths, but this is very undesirable, and would necessitate so much restoration of its walls, steps and cement lining that it would practically be destroyed as a piece of genuine Roman construction.

65 The baths were left open for about fifteen years after they were uncovered before the present cover building was erected.

This was at an early stage in the rebuilding, before the west baths were fully uncovered. Middleton's report provides an interesting comment on the aesthetic susceptibility of the late Victorian antiquaries, who at this time were just beginning to emerge from a period of pseudo-Gothic horror into a new world of airy spaces framed by slender cast iron. In the conflict between 'restoration' and 'minimum modern covering', restoration won. As the visitor can judge for himself today, the results of the partial rebuilding of the Circular Bath are by no means unacceptable.

The first skirmish was of little importance, except to show that the correspondents to the local newspapers were taking a somewhat alarmist view; but in a postscript to his report Middleton adds, 'Since writing the above, further facts have come to my knowledge. Major Davis' scheme includes building new rooms over the hypocaust . . . the walls of which would cut through and practically destroy it.' He adds, in a reference to the reservoir excavation, 'About two years ago the lead plates which wholly lined one of the rectangular tanks were stripped off and sold for old lead by the Corporation . . . I fear it is too late now to stop the mischief which is being done.' Alarmed by this and not entirely in agreement with Middleton's sad concluding remarks a second deputation was sent to Bath on 24 August in the form of no less a person than W. H. St John Hope, Assistant Secretary to the Society of Antiquaries. His report is full of fascinating detail:

I fear that since Mr. Middleton's visit the site had been cleared, and Roman walls laid bare in various directions of a height varying from one or two to five or six feet. They in parts retained their original plastering and appeared in good preservation. Owing to their unequal heights these walls were being levelled up by the workmen with Roman masonry from the debris, and then slate slabs were laid as a damp course and the work carried up in brick. I pointed out to Mr. Davis that if it was necessary to level up the Roman masonry it had better have been done in brick.

Davis evidently did not welcome the advice of outsiders. Later we learn that 'Mr. Davis pointed out a portion of a newly discovered bath . . . which he had instructions to explore, but he said he should give himself no trouble in the matter if interfered with.'

Describing the nature of the work, St John Hope continues:

> On our return to the site of the new works, one of the workmen, in digging a hole for a foundation of a short length of wall to be built against the south wall of the large room already described, came to the original floor on which the hypocaust stands, and although Mr. Davis has assured me that . . . the whole of the hypocaust had perished it now became clear from what the workman laid bare that the *pilae*, at any rate, remained more or less perfect over the whole area of the room. A few feet further west the workmen were clearing away the superficial debris, in order to lay the foundation of a cross wall, and here too the crowbar shewed that the lower floor remained perfect. Mr. Davis thereupon instructed his assistant, Mr. Long, instead of a continuous foundation to build two supporting piers each two feet square upon which the wall could be carried on girders.

In this same spirit of somewhat reluctant compromise the day ended with a heated discussion of the floor levels of the new building, many of which would seal Roman features from view. In his conclusions St John Hope made the following points: that there was no necessity to utilize the old Roman walls; that the new work had been commenced 'for some reason without a proper examination of the site having first been made'; and that,

> though in accordance with Mr. Davis' pledged word to the Society of Antiquaries the Roman work will not *actually* be destroyed, yet a strong personal feeling that has unfortunately been aroused, through the persistent opposition to the proposed plans on account of their destructive character by some of the Roman Antiquaries in Bath, will most certainly end in the whole

of the ancient work being effectually concealed beneath plaster
and concrete and the few trap doors to be provided will be of
no use whatever, and only a concession made to those who desire
that the Roman work should be made accessible for examination.

This was not quite the end of the unhappy story. On 23 November
St John Hope, in the company of the architect Micklethwaite,
returned to the Roman baths 'where we found the Major and a
number of Town Councillors occupied in examining the place'. He
goes on to describe the progress of the building since August, regret-
ting that 'the wall I mentioned as that Mr. Davis ordered to be carried
on piers is built instead on a continuous foundation right across the
area on concrete thrown in, over and around the place which stood
in its line'. The whole tone of this last report is of resigned dissatisfac-
tion. The building was up, protests had been made, but much of
the Roman work had been obscured for years to come.

The events of 1885–6 are of particular interest in showing the
painful beginnings of antiquarian awareness concerning the importance of preserving structures *in situ*. The antiquarians of the mid-
eighteenth century had not raised a whimper when the Duke of
Kingston's Baths were built over the Roman east baths, destroying
much and obscuring the rest. Yet, 130 years later, furious debate was
raging round the problems of best preserving Roman walls for public
view and the ethics of reconstruction. It was something of a turning
point. Davis may have been slack in recording his discoveries and
he may have obscured much by covering the remains with cumbersome and inelegant structures, but a wealth of information remained
beneath his floors, as the excavations of 1969-70 were to show.

The excavations of the mid-1880s were not the end for Davis.
In 1890 he was concerned to expose a large room south of the Circular
Bath, when a new steam laundry was being constructed. And as late
as 1896 a Roman swimming bath was uncovered beneath Stall Street
at the extreme west end of the establishment. Both features were
roofed over but preserved. In sixteen years about two-thirds of the
bathing establishment had been uncovered.

The remaining third, the east end beneath the Duke of Kingston's Bath, finally became available in 1923 when the old baths were demolished. As soon as the superstructure had been removed excavations began under the direction of W. H. Knowles, who had played a key part in the excavations at Corbridge. Knowles was, in fact, the first trained archaeologist to dig in Bath, and his results promptly published in *Archaeologia* bear witness to the fact. At first the workers were disappointed at the massive destruction wrought by the eighteenth-century builders, who had destroyed almost all the late floor-levels at the extreme east end, but as the excavation proceeded this proved to be fortunate, for below were found complex structures of several earlier periods. For the first time it was possible to show that large-scale alterations had taken place during the Roman period. With the east end now open to visitors, nothing more was done for thirty years.

In 1954 Sir Ian Richmond was invited by the Spa Committee to examine the east end of the establishment, in order to make it more intelligible to visitors. This he readily agreed to do, at the same time carrying out a series of limited but elegant excavations, from the results of which he was eventually able to work out the entire structural development of this part of the building. Next he turned his attention to the Great Bath and Circular Bath, and with the same thoroughness and insight by the time of his death in 1965 he had managed to work out the sequence of this central section. Had he lived to finish the work, he would no doubt have completed his study of the entire establishment, but this was not to be and it fell to the Bath Excavation Committee to continue the project by undertaking a detailed re-survey of the western baths, so far as Davis's baths allowed, and by a series of excavations south of the Circular Bath. The work progressed slowly, largely because of the difficulties of cramming excavation beneath and between the pumping equipment which filled the cellars and the need to shift piles of large stone blocks and other rubbish, but by Easter 1968 answers had been obtained to all the major questions.

By this stage the douche and massage baths, erected by Davis amid such furore in 1886, had become derelict and in 1969 the City Council took the decision to demolish them to make way for a new block of shops and offices. The archaeological problems posed were considerable: not only had Davis used Roman walls as his footings, rendering demolition a highly intricate task, but the new building also required foundations of its own which were an immediate threat to the Roman structures. A satisfactory plan of action was, however, soon agreed. Before demolition began trial trenches were dug and

66 Work in progress in 1972 at the west end of the baths, unpicking the concrete foundations, laid by Major Davis in 1886, from around a Roman hypocaust.

Victorian plaster stripped from walls to enable the extent of the Roman work to be established. This done the Roman structures were protected and the walls marked to indicate the maximum extent of permissible demolition. Archaeologists then moved out while the demolition contractors removed the Victorian superstructure. When the last of the rubble had gone the careful work of unpicking the remnants of the nineteenth-century overburden could begin under close archaeological supervision (fig. 66).

Having read the criticisms and controversies surrounding the building of the baths in 1886, we were surprised to find how careful Major Davis had been to preserve the Roman structures. There is little doubt that he did his best, under the most trying conditions, to ensure that his new building not only did the minimum amount of damage but could be removed leaving the Roman walls and floors very much as he had found them. The excavation of 1970–2 enabled the development of the entire west end of the bathing establishment to be studied in full.

The new building was erected using Roman and Victorian walls as foundations, leaving the Roman remains unscathed, and in full view of the public, except where wooden walkways hide small areas of detail. That so much can now be seen is a tribute to the ingenuity of the architects, but that so much remained to be seen we have to thank Major Davis for his care and concern even in the face of a campaign of vitriolic criticism which we now know to have been largely unfounded.

5
THE BATHING ESTABLISHMENT

The central bathing establishment, served by the King's Bath spring, was constructed in the late first century and continued in use into the late fourth or even fifth century, gradually throughout its life undergoing structural modifications, the effects of which were to improve and enlarge the facilities offered to bathers. While it is probable that alterations were continually being made, five main phases can be distinguished.

The initial layout of the baths (Period I) (figure 67)

The baths of the first period were massively constructed in plain bold masonry worthy of the best contemporary work on the Continent. It would appear that the building plan was thought of as three separate units: a spacious hall, with the thermal swimming baths to the east and a suite of artificially heated rooms to the west.

The hall was laid out about a north–south axis emphasized by screen arcades, defining the north and south sides of the central space. Each arcade was composed of massive piers supporting a wide, and proportionally higher, central arch with narrow openings on either

THE BATHING ESTABLISHMENT

67 The baths, period I.

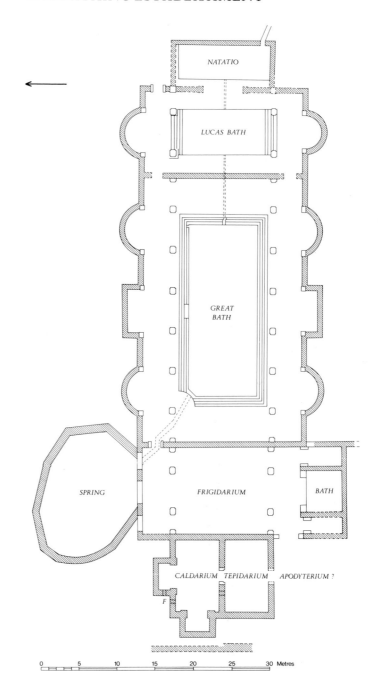

NATATIO

LUCAS BATH

GREAT
BATH

SPRING

FRIGIDARIUM

BATH

CALDARIUM TEPIDARIUM APODYTERIUM ?

F

0   5   10   15   20   25   30 Metres

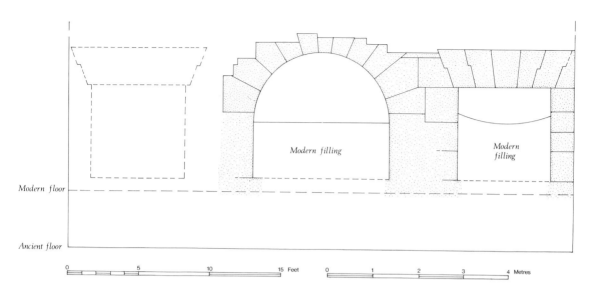

Modern filling

Modern filling

Modern floor

Ancient floor

0   5   10   15 Feet   0   1   2   3   4 Metres

68 The windows in the north wall of the hall overlooking the sacred spring (see figs 36 and 69).

69 One of the square-headed windows in the north wall of the hall. A magnificent example of joggled masonry. (Scale in feet.)

side, and to give an added visual rigidity to the structure the piers were provided with attached pilasters which once supported an architrave and cornice. These internal arrangements were designed so as to focus attention through the north central arch onto the spring and altar beyond, which could be viewed through three large windows perforating the north wall of the hall. The central arched window and the smaller square-headed window next to it with its superb joggled masonry are among the most impressive pieces of Roman architecture surviving in the country (figs 68 and 69). Their very simplicity was contrived to prevent distraction from the view beyond. If the structure of the northern wall of the hall is simple to deduce, that of the southern part is far less clear, due largely to the extensive alterations to which the area was later subjected; but in broad terms a large tank or bath was provided on the central axis framed by a single arched opening, whilst on either side were two short passageways closed by doors for which the monolithic jambs still survive. Since the bath was a cold bath it is best to regard it, together with the hall, as the cold room *(frigidarium)* belonging to the suite of baths to the west. That access was provided in the south west corner suggests that it is in this area, obscured by later buildings, that the main entrance lay. If no special provision had been made here for assembly and undressing then the hall itself is likely to have performed these functions.

Once in the hall, having no doubt admired the view and removed his clothes, the bather was faced with a choice. He could either turn right into the hall which housed the Great Bath, and indulge in a gentle swim in the warm water, or he could turn left towards the suite of Turkish baths for a more rigorous session. The hall, then, served as a place of assembly and at the same time neatly divided the physical atmosphere of the treatments from each other.

Without a doubt, the Great Bath would have been then, as it is now, one of the wonders of Roman Britain (fig. 70). The bath itself lay in the centre of an aisled hall 33.2m long by 20.4m wide, divided into a nave and two side aisles, or ambulatories, by continuous arcades framed with pilasters and entablature like those in the entrance hall. Each ambulatory was provided with three exedrae, a central rectangular recess with semicircular ones on either side, each framed by piers supporting arches in harmony with the main arcades. Clearly they would have formed sitting-out places for those who wished to view the bathing without getting splashed. The hall was entered at its north-west corner from the entrance hall, through a simple opening provided with massive stone door jambs. Stone was used because in such a steam-laden atmosphere wood would quickly have warped. Two other doors were provided, both in the east wall, to give access to a smaller swimming bath, now known as the Lucas Bath, which lay beyond.

Occupying almost the entire central area of the chamber was the Great Bath, a basin 22m by 8.8m sunk to a depth of 1.5m below the floor and reached by four steep steps continuous along all four sides. The entire sunken area was lined with sheets of lead between 1 and 2cms thick and about 3m by 1.5m, laid in three regular rows. Originally the steps would also have been lead-covered, but only a few small fragments which could not be removed because they were wedged behind later blocks now survive. The function of such an elaborate flooring was two-fold: to keep the water in and to prevent the minor springs hereabouts from bubbling up through the bottom. The bath was fed with its main supply of water by a rectangular lead box-pipe leading into the north-west corner and linked directly to the reservoir (fig. 71). A culvert of similar width was provided in the east, side, through which the water passed into the Lucas Bath. For those occasions when it was necessary to drain the bath, or otherwise to regulate the flow, a sluice in the north-east corner could be brought into use to drain water into the main outfall. When the baths were first uncovered, Davis records that this drain was fitted with a bronze sluice, which has since been removed and is now in the museum.

In the general austerity of the hall only a single ornamental feature was provided in the form of a fountain or similar structure set in the centre of the north side of the bath, though it is a distinct possibility that the semicircular arrangement in the north-west corner

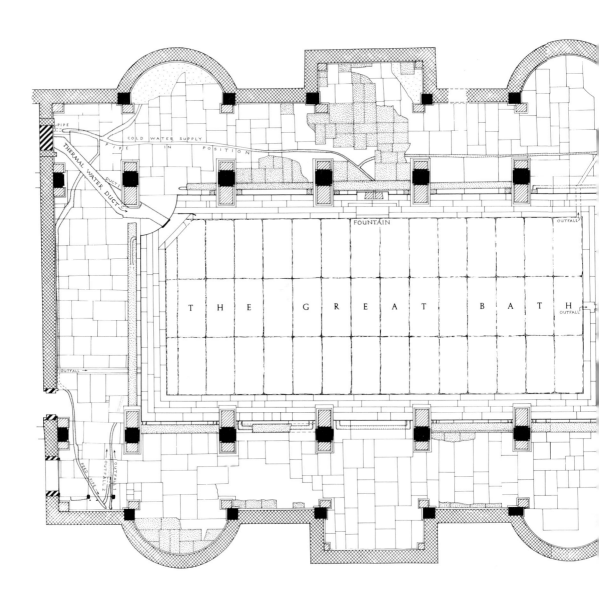

THE GREAT BATH

FOUNTAIN

OUTFALL

OUTFALL

COLD WATER SUPPLY

PIPE IN POSITION

PIPE

THERMAL WATER DUCT

DUCT

OUTFALL

FEED PIPE

OUTFALL 2

OUTFALL 1

0   10   20   30   40   50 Feet

0   5   10   20 Metres

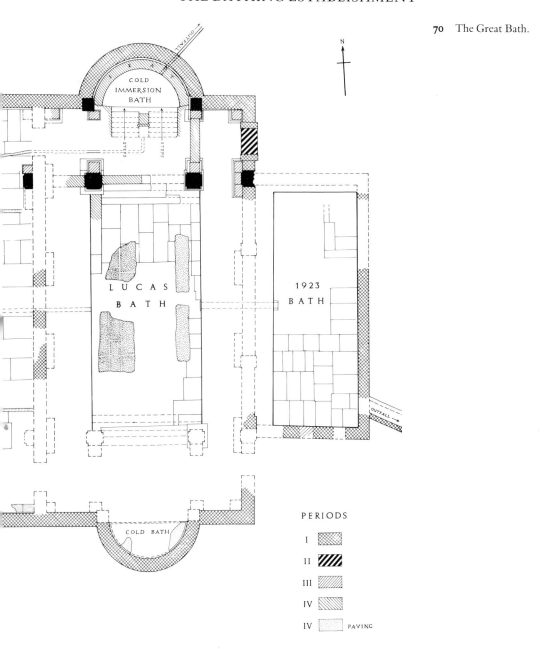

70 The Great Bath.

PERIODS

I

II

III

IV

IV   PAVING

71 The hot mineral water straight from the reservoir entered the Great Bath at its north-west corner over a quadrant-shaped projection which may once have supported an ornamental feature.

of the bath, at the point where the water enters the bath, was also in some way adorned, perhaps with statuary.

In their original state the ambulatories which surrounded the Great Bath were floored with massive slabs of hard white lias limestone, about 20cm thick, most of which are still excellently preserved. Where a considerable volume of water dripping from the bathers would have accumulated on the paving around the edge of the bath between the piers, shallow gutters were cut into the paving, returning at their ends to the edge of the bath to channel the water back.

While we can describe in some detail the ground-plan of the

116

various features, assessment of the superstructure is much more difficult, but the fortunate chance that so much of the collapsed building
has survived in the mud allows the general form, if not the detail,
of the upper part of the hall to be reconstructed. The spacing and
size of the arcade piers and of their attached pilasters demands that
the framing entablature, which the pilasters supported, should be at
a maximum height of 7.3m above the ambulatory (fig. 72). This
much is certain and substantial parts of the entablature, found in the
rubble, allow total reconstruction thus far. What happened above
is much less clear, but since the general proportions of the room

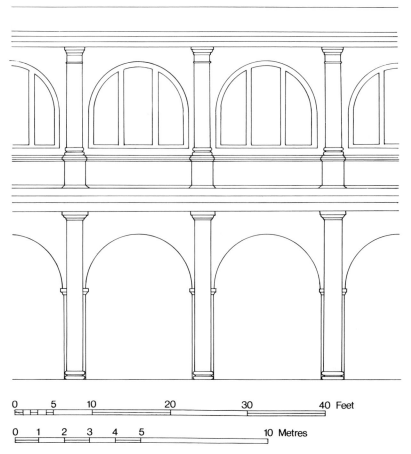

72 Elevation of the Great Bath
arcade in period I.

0   5   10   20   30   40 Feet

0   1   2   3   4   5   10 Metres

117

would require a ceiling at a height of about 13.7m or more to prevent a claustrophobic feeling, there must have been another stage above the lower entablature and moreover a stage which included large lunettes to allow side-light into the chamber. The only fragments of architecture which could have belonged to this second stage are several sections of engaged half-columns, again found by Davis within the rubble filling the hall. One reasonable explanation is that engaged columns were used above the pilasters in the second stage to echo the framing of the lower stage. If so, they would have divided the wall into a series of panels between which would have been semi-circular-headed lunettes matching in proportion the lower arcade. Such an arrangement would have been most effective, as the reconstruction shows: in general conception it was not at all unlike contemporary buildings in Rome, such as the Colosseum.

The roofing of the ambulatories is a much simpler problem. A ceiling with a pitched roof above could easily have been provided on the level of the lower entablature, while the exedrae would have been separately treated. The enclosing wall surfaces were simply plastered with a thick red mortar which originally would have been painted in areas of plain colour.

It will be apparent from the foregoing discussion that the chamber containing the Great Bath was a considerable architectural achievement. Its lines were bold and clean-cut – it was above all a functional building admirably designed to fulfil its purpose. For effect it depended entirely upon the imposing solidity of its masonry and the careful use of volumes and light. No one entering the hall for the first time could have failed to have been impressed by its simple majesty.

Beyond the east wall of the main hall was a smaller chamber, 20.4m long by 10.4m wide, containing the Lucas Bath, first discovered in 1755. Strictly, it was a continuation of the basic structure of the main hall, but its visual axis, like that of the entrance hall, was north–south. In the centre lay the bath, 13.1m by about 6.1m, reached by flights of five steps arranged along the two short sides between the piers. Presumably, like the Great Bath, it would have been lead-lined, but later refloorings have removed all trace. The water supply entered the west side through a culvert connected with the Great Bath and waste water was allowed to drain out of the east side by means of a similar vent leading into yet another bath. The two semicircular recesses with which the ends of the hall were enlivened were probably, like those of the Great Bath, fitted out for relaxing but later alterations have obliterated the earliest arrangement.

The centre of the east wall of the Lucas Bath was pierced by a wide opening leading into a smaller room into which was tightly fitted another bath, measuring 11.9m by 4.4m, discovered by Knowles in 1923. Although it has never been completely excavated, an area of the original stone paving can still be seen in position and in the north-east corner, now refilled, steps were found leading up to the main floor-level. One small fragment of lead still in position shows that this, too, was originally lined with lead. Water was provided by the culvert leading in from the Lucas Bath, while the main outfall led from the south-east corner. Visually the Lucas Bath and 1923 bath functioned together, the 1923 bath appearing simply as a basin in an alcove opening out of the side of the Lucas Bath chamber. The opening was probably framed by a simple arch set behind an engaged entablature in the manner of the main hall. While the Lucas Bath would have been roofed in the same way as the Great Bath, the 1923 bath may well have been enclosed with a lower ceiling probably on the level of the main entablature. Thus the thermal bath-range consisted of swimming baths decreasing in size, grandeur and temperature.

Returning, now, to the other end of the establishment, the heated baths on the west side of the hall were altogether different in function and architecture. The rooms were smaller and each was designed for a specific purpose. It seems likely that access to the suite was provided from the hall by means of a southern corridor (now obscured by later features), from which the bather would normally pass into the adjacent *tepidarium* (warm room). Although the *tepidarium* was later refloored at a higher level, the general arrangement in the first period must have been much the same as it later became, with hot air coming in through vents in the north wall, into a basement created by supporting the main floor on regularly spaced piers of tiles (*pilae*). After circulating in this space the air passed into a jacketing of vertical box-tiles attached to the walls of the room, which led out through chimneys in the roof. The rising of the hot air through the wall flues created the draught necessary to draw more hot air into the basement hypocaust, thus maintaining the flow. The later floor of this room incorporated the further refinement of hollow box-tile jacketing within the thickness of the floor. Such an arrangement would have made a far more efficient use of the hot air but we cannot be certain that the same system was employed in the first period.

Through a wide door in the north wall of the *tepidarium* lay the *caldarium* (hot room), of similar size. Although the drastic remodelling of the fourth period has completely destroyed the original fittings, there can be little doubt that the floor would have been constructed in much the same way as that of the *tepidarium*, with the hot air supplied by a flue opening through the north wall. The room was provided with two large recesses, each of which was fitted out with small plunge baths heated from below and no doubt served with hot water from a boiler above the main stokery to the north.

The use of these rooms is clear. Having first undressed, probably in the hall, the bather would have entered the *tepidarium*, a room of gentle heat designed to prepare the body for more vigorous treatment. After a while he would have passed into the hot steamy atmosphere of the *caldarium*, where he could choose between sitting in the main room or bathing in the hot plunges provided in the alcoves. It may well be that these were so arranged that one was hotter than the other, allowing the bather to work up gradually to the hottest treatment. When the spell in the 'Turkish' bath was over, the body would be allowed to cool off gradually by passing slowly through the *tepidarium*. Finally, the treatment would be completed with a swim in the cold bath set in the alcove in the south side of the hall.

No certain evidence survives as to the nature of the roof of this part of the building. There would have been no need for the high spaces provided for the thermal baths to the east where height was a positive advantage to allow the steam from the thermal water to rise. In the heated range quite the reverse was true, as relatively low ceilings would have been required to retain the hot, steamy atmosphere. Since wooden structures were quite useless in baths of this kind (the wood would have warped and there would have been constant danger from fire), the two heated rooms must have been vaulted with concrete and box-tiles, presumably in two parallel east–west tunnel vaults. It will never be known whether the vaults were left as bare concrete, as they were in the famous Hunting Baths at Lepcis Magna, or if they were covered with pitched slated roofs, rather more suitable for a rainy climate. The side corridors were, however, almost certainly covered with simple pitched roofs.

As we have shown, it is possible to describe the original bathing establishment in considerable detail, not only as a ground-plan but also in terms of its function and superstructure. It remains to say something of its date. On archaeological grounds there is very little evidence. A limited excavation south of the entrance hall produced a few fragments of late first- or early second-century pottery from a lens of soil which had accumulated over the building spread contemporary with the initial construction, suggesting the possibility of a late first-century date, but this is hardly conclusive. Nor can much be said on architectural grounds. The style of the building in its bold simplicity defies accurate dating, but it would not have been out of place in late first-century Rome, where several buildings in a similar vein were being erected. The inscriptions found in Bath from time to time throw some light on the problem. Several of them, put up by visitors to the spa, are of first-century date and since people are unlikely to have made the journey to visit a bubbling marsh, the implication is that the Baths were in existence at this time. Finally, it is to the late first century that the first series of massive monumental urban building in Britain belongs. Civic authorities were receiving official encouragement from the government for their building programmes – Bath may have been one of them.

73 The baths, period II.

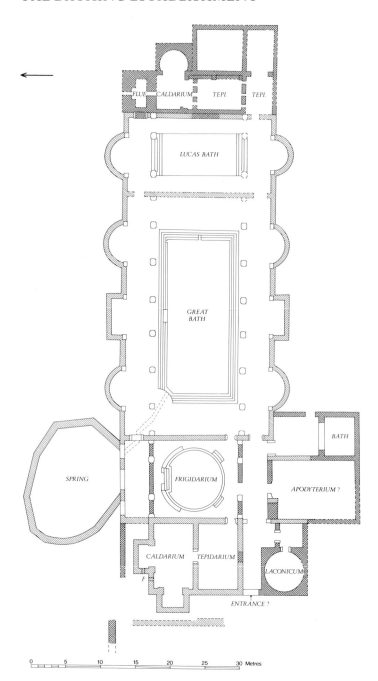

Within the plan:

FLUE   CALDARIUM   TEPI.   TEPI.

LUCAS BATH

GREAT BATH

SPRING

FRIGIDARIUM

BATH

APODYTERIUM ?

CALDARIUM   TEPIDARIUM

LACONICUM

F

ENTRANCE ?

0   5   10   15   20   25   30 Metres

The first extension to the bathing establishment (Period II) (figure 73)

At a time not long after the original building was put up, major alterations were undertaken at both the east and west ends to improve the range of facilities offered to bathers. At the east end the 1923 bath and its alcove were dismantled and the inlet which fed it from the Lucas Bath was joined to the outlet by a stone-built culvert running diagonally across the bath (fig. 74): it can still be seen in a tolerably well-preserved state. Having thus re-arranged the drainage system the old bath was filled with rubble; its original walls were thickened by new internal foundations, the added strength being needed

74 When the easternmost plunge bath of the original establishment was no longer needed, a culvert was built across its floor to drain away waste water and the entire bath was filled with rubble to form the basis for a new suite of heated baths. (Scale in feet.)

123

to support the heavy vaulted superstructure. Further extensions were made to the south and east. The resulting suite was very much like the arrangement of the early 'Turkish' baths at the west end.

The visitor, entering through a small door in the south-east corner of the Lucas Bath chamber, would find himself in a pair of gently warmed rooms leading to a large 6m square undressing room. Returning through the passage he would enter the *tepidarium*, built over the old 1923 bath, warmed to a higher temperature by means of hot air entering the hypocausts from the *caldarium* to the north. As soon as he was acclimatized he would have proceeded into the *caldarium*, a rectangular room with a large semicircular bath opening from one wall. The high temperature of the room was maintained by a massive flue immediately to the north, which produced both the hot air circulating beneath the floor and a plentiful supply of hot water from a boiler which would have been constructed over the flue. At the end of the steam treatment he would have cooled his body gradually by passing through the *tepidarium*, probably completing the session with a gentle swim in the tepid water of the Lucas Bath before returning to the changing toom.

The superstructure of the new baths is easy to reconstruct theoretically. The range of heated rooms, and probably the flue as well, would have been covered with a simple barrel-vault arranged on a north–south axis, while the semicircular bath of the *caldarium* would have been provided with a semi-dome. The undressing room and the passage to the south were probably protected by a pitched roof.

The alterations at the west end were altogether more far-reaching (fig. 75), but, simply stated, a new type of bathing facility was inserted into the area between the Great Bath and the eastern range of 'Turkish' baths. The central element of the new treatment was a large circular room known as a *laconicum*, which would have been heated by means of a flue in the south wall to a very high temperature indeed. Since it was *dry* heat that was required, the *laconicum* was isolated from the rest of the baths to prevent contamination from the general steamy atmosphere. Next to it a large court was created by the obliteration of the first-period bath and corridors, south of

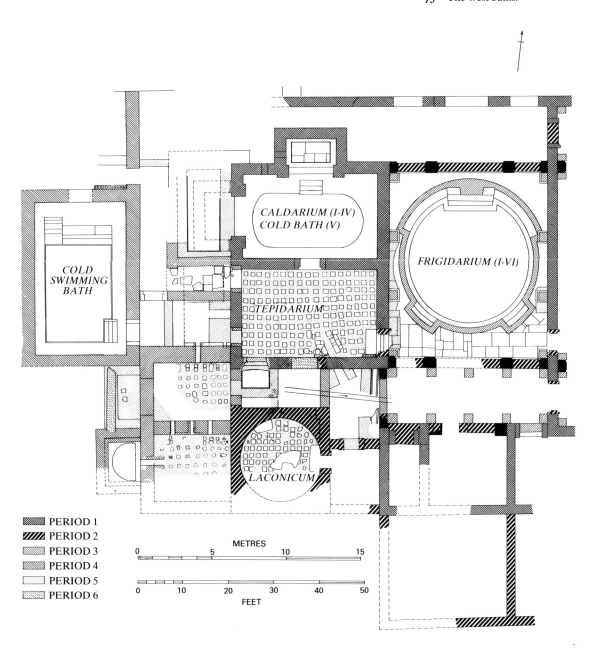

75 The west baths.

COLD
SWIMMING
BATH

CALDARIUM (I-IV)
COLD BATH (V)

FRIGIDARIUM (I-VI)

TEPIDARIUM

LACONICUM

PERIOD 1
PERIOD 2
PERIOD 3
PERIOD 4
PERIOD 5
PERIOD 6

METRES
0   5   10   15

0   10   20   30   40   50
FEET

125

the entrance hall, and by further extension to the south. The newly defined area was paved with large slabs of limestone. Its function is uncertain. While it is most likely to have been an undressing room (*apodyterium*), the possibility that it may have been an exercise court should not be ruled out. It was conveniently placed, opening off the main east–west corridor which would have led from the main entrance at the west end of the establishment to a new doorway cut in the west wall of the Great Bath chamber.

The third element of the new arrangement consisted of a circular plunge bath nearly 9m in diameter and 1.2m deep, which was fitted rather tightly into the central area of the entrance hall. The bath was provided with steps of massive masonry leading down from the surrounding paved area to its floor, which originally was probably of lead-covered stone flags, but now only the rubble foundation survives. Into the north side of the bath projects a platform which would once have supported an ornamental fountain supplying cold water. The overflow can still be seen leading out of the south-east corner into an extensive series of sewers which eventually drain into a culvert running along the south side of the establishment into the main drain.

Alterations as extensive as these necessarily caused a displacement and reorganization of the other facilities. The old hall, now containing the Circular Bath, was walled across between the arcade piers on the north and south sides. With the exception of a single doorway in the south, the walls were probably taken up to fill the arcades completely. This would have meant that the view across the spring was now destroyed, but it is a distinct possibility that the corridor to the north of the Circular Bath was refloored at a higher level to serve as a viewing platform for the spring, reached by steps from the north ambulatory of the Great Bath or direct from the temple precinct. In fact, much the same as the present arrangement. An interesting piece of evidence to support this suggestion is that the north-facing sides of the two piers were enlivened with fluting (fig. 76), which stops not at the original first-period floor but at the new platform level with which the tooling is likely to be contemporary. Clearly the view *into* the baths from the temple was important.

126

Additional access to the baths was now provided through a new entrance hall attached to the south-west corner of the Great Bath chamber, which opened into what was originally the south-west corner of the old hall but was now a passageway linking various elements

76 The piers in the entrance hall were massive. Those which would have been seen by someone looking into the hall from the temple precinct were fluted. (Scale in feet.)

127

of the establishment. The new entrance hall was provided with a large bath opening out of the south wall and replacing functionally the closely similar bath that was filled up to make way for the *apodyterium*. The whole area is now heavily cluttered with derelict machinery and rubbish, but nevertheless some limited excavation was possible. This showed that the bath was originally floored with large limestone flagstones which had later been covered with a thick coating of red mortar continuous with the rendering of the walls and steps leading to it. It is very much to be hoped that one day the whole of this important area will be cleared and put on display. Why a subsidiary entrance should have been provided here is not immediately apparent, but one explanation is that it provided access to an exercise yard south of the Great Bath.

Having described the extensive additions and alterations, we must now consider how the new suite was intended to function. After undressing in the *apodyterium*, it is likely that the exercise was taken to tone up the muscles and produce a pleasant tiredness. Then the bather would enter the *laconicum*, sitting first of all low down and gradually (if the facility were provided) moving to a higher tier of seats where the atmosphere would be much hotter. The *laconicum* functioned, in fact, in exactly the same way as a modern Scandinavian sauna bath, the intense dry heat of the bath promoting profuse sweating. A period in the enervating atmosphere would be immediately followed by a sharp plunge in the cold water of the Circular Bath. Finally, the bather could choose between returning to the entrance hall to dress or a gentle swim in the warm water of the Great Bath before finally emerging from the establishment.

It will be evident from the plan that the construction of the 'sauna' baths cut off the access to the western range of 'Turkish' baths. To overcome this difficulty, two new doors were cut in the east and west walls of the Circular Bath chamber, thus providing a direct route between the Great Bath and the *tepidarium*. A bather wishing to take a 'Turkish bath', on entering and changing, would proceed through to the chamber containing the Circular Bath to the *tepidarium* and eventually the *caldarium* before returning to the Circular Bath for a cold dip. Thus the Circular Bath now served as the cold plunge for both sauna and Turkish treatments.

The exact date at which these changes took place is difficult to define and indeed we cannot be certain that they were all of one period, but the similarity of the masonry at both the east and west ends suggests that both sets of alterations are broadly contemporary and the fact that the *laconicum* is detached hints at a date no later than the middle of the second century. Of the few scraps of pottery found beneath the contemporary building spread on the south side of the baths, none dates to after the first quarter of the second century. Therefore the evidence, such as it is, would allow the alterations to have taken place during the reign of Hadrian.

To summarize the whole range of second-period alterations, it may be said that they were designed to enlarge greatly the facilities offered to the public. In addition to the original thermal swimming baths and range of 'Turkish' baths, a second set of 'Turkish' baths was added, together with the rather more specialized 'sauna' baths. Why two 'Turkish' establishments were required is not clear. One possibility is that instead of opening at different times for males and females, as was frequently the practice at this time, the establishment was now rearranged so that both sexes could use the building at the same time. By closing the door between the Circular Bath and *tepidarium*, the western 'Turkish' baths could have been completely isolated from the rest of the establishment, thus maintaining propriety. The theory, however possible, must remain completely speculative.

Rebuilding and re-roofing (Period III) (figure 77)

At some stage during the late second or early third century the decision was taken to extend the establishment and to re-roof it completely, probably because the original timber roof, which by this time might well have been about a hundred years old, had warped and rotted in the damp atmosphere. The answer was to re-roof entirely with masonry with an enormous barrel-vault sprung from the side arcades. Such a project necessarily entailed the considerable strength-

77 The baths, period III.

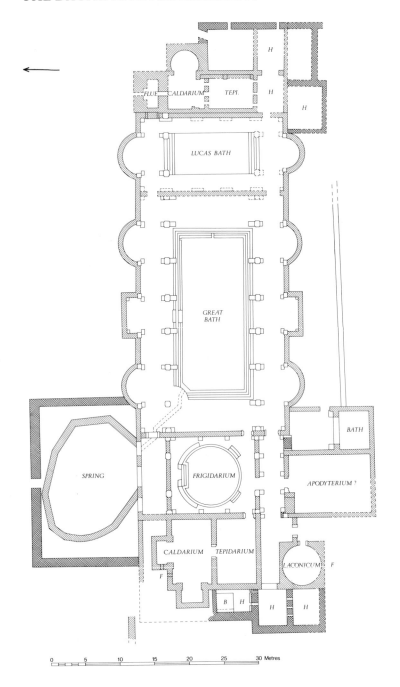

FLUE CALDARIUM TEPI.

H

H

H

LUCAS BATH

GREAT
BATH

BATH

SPRING

FRIGIDARIUM

APODYTERIUM ?

CALDARIUM TEPIDARIUM

LACONICUM F

F

B H

H H

0 5 10 15 20 25 30 Metres

ening of the supporting foundations and the creation of buttressing masses to absorb the newly-created lateral thrusts. The foundations are fortunately so well preserved that the details of the work can be closely followed.

In the hall containing the Great Bath the arcade piers were considerably strengthened by cutting back the base moulds of the engaged pilasters and extending them by adding new bases to the front and back (fig. 79). The external walls of the chamber were also strength-

78 The Great Bath empty of water showing the sheets of lead lining the bottom. The modern colonnaded ambulatory does not reproduce in any way the original Roman appearance.

ened with new piers added to those which framed the alcoves and by the addition of further piers to the inner angles of the rectangular alcoves (fig. 80). Although superficially the new work might be thought to alter the internal appearance of the hall, the lower stage, and quite probably the upper, would not have looked very different – the same proportions and detailing could easily have been retained in front of a greatly strengthened substructure. The main difference lay in the nature of the roof itself, for the original ceiling, presumably of coffered timber work, was now replaced by a somewhat higher

79 When the Great Bath was vaulted with masonry in the third period, the main piers, which had hitherto supported the timber roof, had to be considerably strengthened to take the increased weight. (Scale in feet.)

concrete vault open at both ends to allow the steam to escape (fig. 81). Large fragments of the vault found within the rubble filling the bath show that it was constructed of hollow box-tiles, to reduce the weight, capped with a covering of concrete and tiles. The open ends, one of which still survives and is displayed in the baths (fig. 82), were neatly finished with a tiled facing to the *intrados* and horizontally-coursed tiles above.

The haunches of the main vault rested on the arcades which, as we have seen, were strengthened to take the greatly increased vertical thrusts. Since the ambulatories would have been roofed with continuous tunnel-vaults at normal ceiling level or a little higher, the lateral thrusts to which the piers were subjected would have been dissipated by the buttressing effect of the ambulatory structure.

80 To strengthen the side walls of the Great Bath when the vaulted roof was built, additional piers were added to absorb the lateral thrust. (Scale in feet.)

133

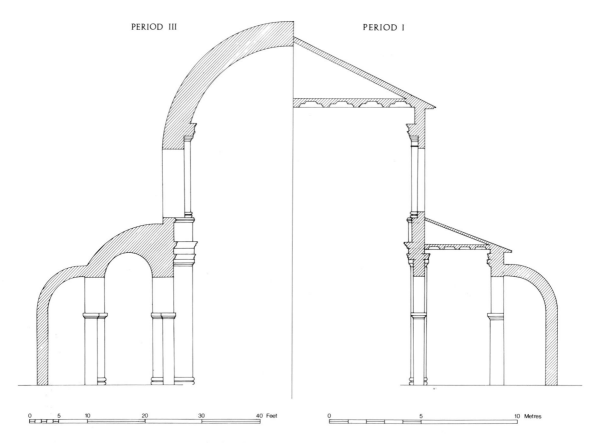

PERIOD III　　　　　　　　　　　　　　　　PERIOD I

0　5　10　　　20　　　30　　　40 Feet

0　　　　　　　　　5　　　　　　　　10 Metres

81 Sections across the Great Bath showing how the masonry was strengthened when the roof was vaulted.

Further buttressing was provided by the exedrae. The beautiful simplicity of the whole structural concept is shown best by the section (fig. 81).

While there is no doubt that the vault of the Great Bath lay east–west, the arrangement over the Lucas Bath is a little less certain. Strictly, it could have been vaulted with a continuation of the main vault, but the strengthening of the north-south walls of the chamber, with supports for blind arcades, is a strong indication that in this instance its axis ran north–south, the blind arcade being necessary to take the additional weight for which the walls were not originally designed. One positive advantage of such an arrangement was that it allowed the east end of the Great Bath vault to remain open without

134

hindrance. Whether or not the ends of the Lucas Bath vault were also open cannot easily be assessed. The presence of the apsidal *exedrae*, however, would have demanded semi-domes which argue against open ends.

The Circular Bath and the corridors on either side of it were also vaulted at this time. The southern corridor, which served as the main thoroughfare linking the 'sauna' baths to the Great Bath, was specially treated with a long east–west tunnel-vault, supported on a blind arcade still remarkably well-preserved (figs. 83 and 84). In one place a complete pier survives with two voussoir stones of the arch still in position on the capital. The Circular Bath chamber, like that of the Lucas Bath, was provided with a north–south vault springing from newly-built blind arcades fitted rather awkwardly

82 The vault which covered the Great Bath was open at both ends to allow the steam to escape. One of the tile-built facings still survives. (Scale in feet.)

135

into the space between the bath and the side walls. Presumably the same vault was carried over the corridor to the north. Both ends would necessarily have been open to admit light.

The effect of these third-position alterations was to enclose completely the central elements of the bathing establishment with masonry. The skilful use of blind arcading to thicken the load-bearing walls caused minimum disruption to the existing superstructure: as far as possible the new features were constructed within the shell of the old without large-scale demolition. But in spite of the careful planning, the central part of the baths must have been out of commission for a considerable time whilst the vault was being erected. Enormous amounts of timber shuttering and scaffolding would have been required to build the frame over which the vaults were laid, completely choking the baths. It would have remained for some time whilst the concrete was setting, until the architect in charge finally took the decision to remove it. It must have been an agonizing period to live through: waiting to see if the calculations had been correct and the materials strong enough, as the whole structure settled together in a new complex of carefully balanced thrusts and tensions.

83 Diagram of the blind arcading added south of the Circular Bath to strengthen the walls.

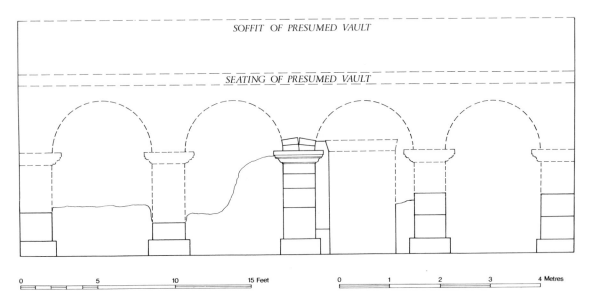

SOFFIT OF PRESUMED VAULT

SEATING OF PRESUMED VAULT

| 0 | 5 | 10 | 15 Feet |

| 0 | 1 | 2 | 3 | 4 Metres |

84 One of the well preserved piers of the blind arcade added to the corridor south of the Circular bath in period III.

At about the same time alterations were being carried out on the heated baths at both ends. At the east end the changing room of the earlier period and the smaller room to the south were completely remodelled . The east wall was rebuilt on a more massive scale and both rooms were now provided with hypocausts heated by means of flues opening through the east wall. At least two more heated rooms were now added to the south. The general effect of these changes was to increase the number of *caldaria* in which the bathers could sweat profusely before swimming in the curative waters of the Great Bath or Lucas Bath. Thus it was the curative facilities of the baths that were now being extended. The rebuilding of the east wall on a more massive scale is an interesting indication that now that the easternmost range of rooms was heated, it was thought desirable to replace its roof with a vault to reduce the hazard of fire.

Alterations and additions were also being undertaken to the south of the Great Bath. The second-period entranceway into the south-east corner of the old entrance hall was now blocked up and various minor additions were made to the bath which opened out of the south wall of the second-period hall. Clearly these rooms were no longer a functional part of the ranges to the north. It is, however, a distinct possibility that they now formed part of a new south range, about which practically nothing is known, perhaps linked to the southwards extension of the east baths described above. Between these two southward projections runs a stylobate of massive stone blocks supporting a full-scale colonnade, some of the bases of which still survive in position. The columns would have taken a sloping verandah roof resting against a wall to the south. While it is likely that this constituted the entire structure hereabouts, the southern wall being the limit of the establishment, it is just possible that what we are seeing is the north-facing verandah of a large, as yet undefined, building to the south. Only further excavation will provide the answers.

One interesting change took place at a later date: the bases of the columns were cut back and a series of curious massively-framed window mouldings were inserted between them, serving to isolate the verandah from the open area to the north. One of the mouldings still survives in position.

At the west end there were further modifications. It seems that the main entrance was resited between the *laconicum* and *apodyterium* so that a suite of three new heated rooms could be built abutting the west wall of the establishment. The central room, opening directly from the access corridor, may have been little more than a heated lobby serving the other two. The room to the north was provided with a small sunken heated bath and it is quite possible that the southern room was similarly fitted out. The facility is clearly additional to those already provided at the west end and it is tempting to see it as the first suite of curative immersion baths to be built in Bath.

The structural changes of this third period can now be seen to have been largely concerned with re-roofing on a large scale. Such alterations to the ground-plan as there were, to the baths at either end, were of a relatively minor nature. Dating is even more difficult than with the earlier periods, indeed the only fragment of evidence is a coin of Hadrian which was found mortared to one of the additional piers in the Great Bath. All that can safely be said is that the third period alterations post-date the reign of Hadrian.

The re-organization of the bathing facilities (Period IV) (figure 85)

The re-organization following some years after the great period of re-roofing was on a very large scale, creating at the east end (fig. 86) the most impressive suite of heated rooms ever to be built at Bath. This was accomplished quite simply by demolishing the *tepidarium*, *caldarium* and flue of the second period, which had served until now, and replacing them with two vast new rooms measuring 6.7m by 11.3m. The southern room, which functioned as a *tepidarium*, was without internal elaborations, but the northern room, the *caldarium*, was fitted with a pair of fine semicircular baths floored with simple mosaic pavements. Between them was a large flue for providing the

85 The baths, period IV.

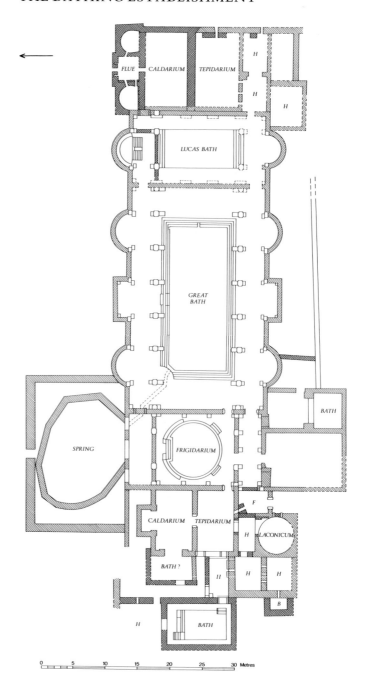

FLUE | CALDARIUM | TEPIDARIUM | H | H

LUCAS BATH

GREAT BATH

SPRING | FRIGIDARIUM | BATH

CALDARIUM | TEPIDARIUM | F | H | LACONICUM

BATH ? | H | H | H

H | BATH | B

0 5 10 15 20 25 30 Metres

86 The east baths.

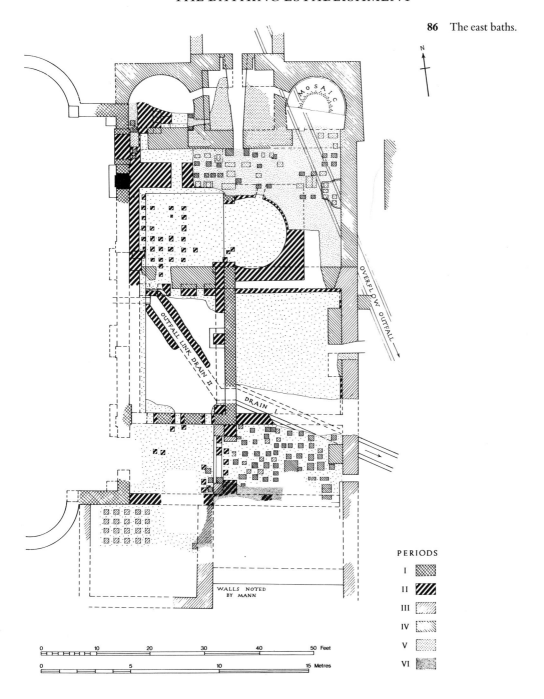

WALLS NOTED
BY MANN

MOSAIC

OVERFLOW OUTFALL

OUTFALL LINK DRAIN II

DRAIN I

		Feet
0 10 20 30 40 50		Feet
0 5 10	15	Metres

PERIODS

I	
II	
III	
IV	
V	
VI	

87 Fragment of a late hypocaust still preserved in the east baths. (Scale in feet.)

88 The ambulatories surrounding the Great Bath were paved with slabs of limestone 20cm thick. Late in the life of the establishment a new lead water-pipe was inserted in a slot cut into the slabs and a new paving was laid above. The lead pipe and patches of the second floor still survive. (Scale in feet.)

hot air for the hypocaust of the *caldarium* itself as well as for the hypocausts below the semicircular baths. It was these floors that the antiquarians of 1755 were recording, but very little survived the construction of the Kingston Baths.

The chamber containing the Lucas Bath underwent a series of interesting alterations at about this time. The northern alcove was walled off from the main room and made accessible only from the north ambulatory of the Great Bath. The floor of the alcove was then considerably lowered and a new floor laid at a depth of 1.2m with a stone bench around the curve of the apse. The floor was reached by a flight of steps from the centre of which projected a stone culvert supplying water. The purpose of the new arrangement is clear: the alcove was converted into a curative immersion bath in which the patient sat immersed up to the neck in the healing water. Treatment of this kind was popular in Rome ever since the Emperor Augustus was cured in this way by the physician Antonius Musa.

142

The water for the new bath was provided directly from the sacred spring through a lead pipe which ran along the north ambulatory of the Great Bath, branching at one point to serve a fountain on the north side of the bath. The lead pipe is still remarkably preserved for part of its length and the channel in which it was laid can be traced as a slot cut into the paving slabs (figs 88 and 89). It was probably immediately after this that the ambulatory floor surrounding the Great Bath was completely repaved with lias slabs, covering the water pipes from view. One further detail can be added: the south alcove of the Lucas Bath chamber was also provided with a sunken bath lined with waterproof pink mortar. Although it is impossible to be sure when the change was made, it could be broadly of this period.

At the west end far-reaching alterations were also being undertaken. A totally new cold plunge bath was built, immediately adjacent to the existing baths beyond the west wall. It was associated with a new suite of heated rooms, to the north, about which little is known because they lie beneath an unexcavated part of Stall Street. To reach this new facility access had to be extensively reorganized, the original, period I *tepidarium* now serving as a heated vestibule. One doorway led through another heated corridor direct to the new cold plunge: another gave access to a narrow corridor leading to the new heated suite, while a third, in the south wall, opened into a heated vestibule leading to the rooms added in period III and also, through a new door, to the *laconicum*. These complexities are best appreciated by reference to the plan (fig. 85). At the same time all the earlier hypocausts were gutted and rebuilt at a higher level, the old *tepidarium* (fig. 90) was provided with a new flue in its south wall, a small hot bath was added to the period III heated room and the west bath of the old *caldarium* was completely rebuilt.

The overall effect of this extensive refurbishment at the west end was to greatly extend the facilities but since the entire plan has not yet been recovered it is difficult to appreciate the underlying logic of the arrangement. For the bather, however, the maze of corridors and plethora of doors must have been more than a little confusing.

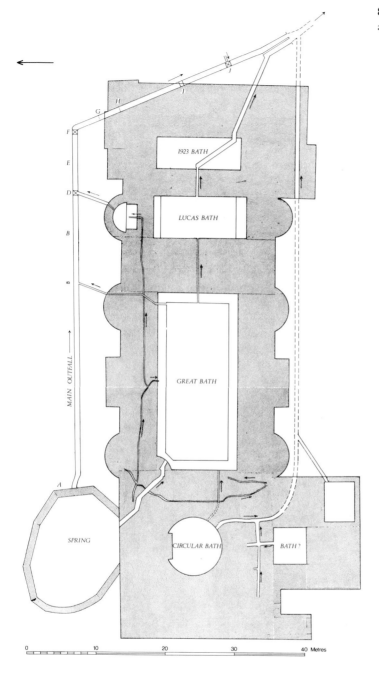

89 Diagram to show the drains and water supply of the baths.

MAIN OUTFALL →

1923 BATH

LUCAS BATH

GREAT BATH

SPRING

CIRCULAR BATH

BATH?

0   10   20   30   40 Metres

145

146

The final alterations (Periods V and VI)

It was in the fifth period that the western baths reached their final form. The old *caldarium*, which had served from period I, was now dismantled and an oval-ended oblong swimming bath was inserted to serve as a cold bath (fig. 91). The little bath attached to the north side now also became a cold pool while the warm bath in the west alcove was walled across and now opened only to the west. As part of this programme of renovation the old *tepidarium* was supplied with an additional source of heat from a new stokery beyond its west wall, and a new small heated bath was added to the south. The small baths attached to the heated rooms west of the *laconicum* were also refitted.

90 The west baths after Major Davis's 1886 douche and massage baths had been removed and before the new office building was erected above. The hypocaust of the main *tepidarium* is well preserved.

91 The west baths (with part of Major Davis's baths still in position). The oval-ended cold bath was inserted into the original *caldarium* late in the life of the establishment.

Although these alterations were comparatively minor, and were undertaken without dislocating the superstructure, the loss of the *caldarium* must have detracted from the comfort of the facilities even though the increased heat supply to the *tepidarium* may have been intended to compensate.

At the east end changes were altogether more drastic. It seems that the hypocaust basements were now suffering from periods of flooding (p. 211) and to counteract this the basement floor-levels were raised by about 22cm with puddled clay rammed between the pilae. Though superficially of a minor nature, the work would have entailed the removal of all suspended floors and their subsequent replacement. At about this time, the flue was partly blocked to support a new hot-water boiler, which meant that the semicircular baths could no longer be heated direct from the flue. Provision had to be made, therefore, to provide hot air from the *caldarium*. In a final sixth phase, the hypocaust at the south end of the east baths was finally abandoned, the room being refloored with hard pink mortar.

These are the last definable alterations before the flooding became so serious that the establishment had to be abandoned, and the centre of Bath reverted once more to a marsh.

6
THE ROMAN TOWN OF BATH

The title of this chapter begs one of the biggest outstanding questions concerning the archaeology of Bath: in the Roman period, was the settlement a town or simply a collection of religious buildings and bathing establishments? Before we can begin to attempt an answer it is necessary to offer a brief survey of the other Roman buildings outside the vast central temple and baths complex to see if this evidence in any way points to the true nature of the settlement.

Public building east of the temple (figure 13)

Immediately to the east of the temple and north of the bathing establishment Davis discovered, but did not properly record, massive foundations, some of which are now exposed beneath the floors of the museum. According to Richard Mann's notes, a Roman concrete platform overlaid the walls, but much of it had suffered from robbing in the eighteenth century and the rest was destroyed in the building programme of 1893. Although the surviving fragments are too few to give any clear idea of the function of the building to which they belong, there is no doubt at all that it was of monumental character.

From its position there are two possibilities: either it was part of a great forum and basilica arrangement, or it was the stage area of a theatre. In Gaul both types of buildings were frequently found in central positions arranged adjacent to, and on the same axis as, large temples. Architecturally neither would be out of context here in Bath but it must be admitted that there is no structural evidence available to decide between the possibilities, and the proximity of the abbey rules out decisive excavation. If the foundations were part of a theatre, then both theatre and temple components would have functioned closely together, as they did in Gaul, the theatre often being used for the continuation of ritual performances. The combination of theatre, temple and bathing establishment would have made Bath a religious, curative and recreational centre without parallel in the country.

On the other hand the foundations could well be part of a monumental courtyard, either a forum or another sacred precinct, and it is tempting to suggest that here may have been sited the ornate *tholos*, or circular shrine, some fragments of which were found lying among the rubble tipped into the east end of the Great Bath. The surviving blocks represent the frieze and cornice of the monument. They were carved on both their outer and inner faces. The inner surface was ornamented with a continuous leafy scroll (fig. 92), while the more important outer face was divided into a series of panels of varying sizes containing small draped figures separated by panels of foliage. The monument was evidently one of considerable pretension and must rank among the most important structures of Roman Bath.

The Westgate Street monument

The fragments, described here rather grandly as 'the Westgate Street monument', are even more elusive of interpretation than the supposed theatre courtyard. All that now remain are four fragments of sculptured cornice from a gigantic monument, which came to light in 1869 during the rebuilding of the Pump Room Hotel; needless to say, it was James Irvine who was responsible for their preservation.

92 Several blocks, carved with elaborate motifs, found in the rubble filling the baths constitute part of a circular building, probably a shrine, which may have stood in the courtyard east of the temple precinct. The frieze has a continuous tendril motif on the inner face, while the outer face is carved in panels containing human figures and floral designs. Height 46cm.

The largest fragment is part of an elaborately sculptured cornice in the centre of which is set a larger-than-life-sized face of apparently human form, serving as a gargoyle to disperse the rainwater accumulating in a gutter cut into the upper surface (fig. 93). The other, smaller, pieces probably belonged to the same entablature. There are also in the general collection of carved stone from the central area of Bath several fragments of a Corinthian capital of similar proportions, which may possibly belong to the same structure. Compared

93 The cornice of a massive monumental building found in Westgate Street. It bears human heads, which act as gargoyles, carved at intervals between formal fleur-de-lis type motifs. Height 46.5cm.

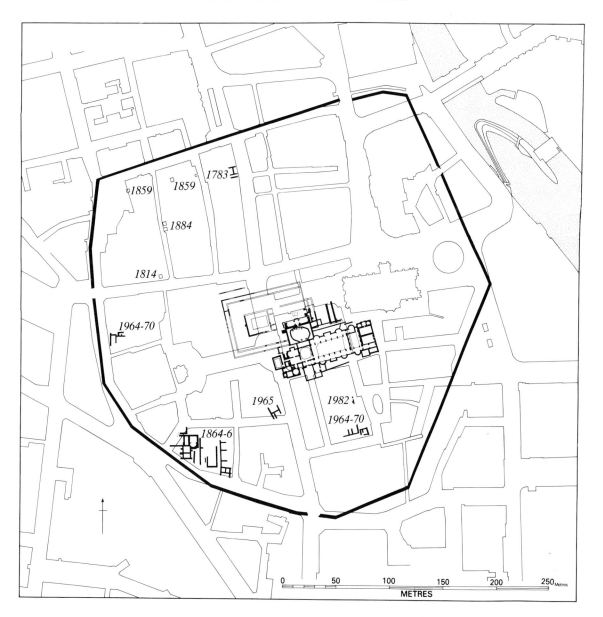

94 General plan of the walled area of Roman Bath.

with the cornice of the temple, this monument must have been about twice as large.

The Hot Baths (figures 95 to 97)

There is no doubt that the spring which served the main bathing establishment was the hottest and most copious source in the settlement, but there were two other subsidiary springs in the south-west corner of the enclosed area, one now serving the Hot Baths and another the Cross Bath. Both were used during the Roman period.

Between 1864 and 1866 an area of land between Hot Bath Street and Beau Street was redeveloped for the new Royal United Hospital. Fortunately the building programme coincided with Irvine's resi-

95 The south-west corner of the town.

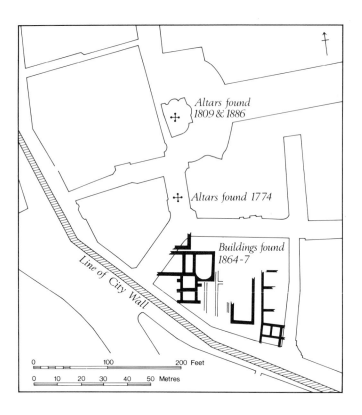

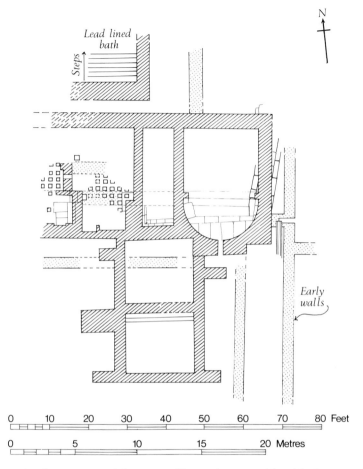

N

96 Plan of the Roman Hot Baths redrawn after J. T. Irvine.

Lead lined bath

Steps

Early walls

0   10   20   30   40   50   60   70   80 Feet

0   5   10   15   20 Metres

dence in the town and he naturally took a considerable interest in the progress of the work, over the years producing his usual meticulous plans as well as a delightful photograph (fig. 97). His discoveries were of some significance. He was able to show that an early Roman building of undefined function and date was demolished and superseded by an elaborate suite of baths apparently consisting of two separate sections, a heated range and a swimming bath. Of the heated range, the excavations exposed a large *caldarium* (?) with an apsidal bath in one end, separated by a corridor from a further *caldarium* or *tepidarium* with its floor supported on *pilae*. Evidently there had

155

97 The building of the Royal United Hospital in 1867 brought to light parts of two Roman buildings, one a bathing establishment part of which is seen in this contemporary photograph.

been considerable alteration in this part of the range, but the exact sequence and details are no longer clear, nor is it possible to assess the functions of the two other rooms which were linked to the corridor.

Of the plunge bath, only the corner lay within the area available for excavation (fig. 97), but enough survived to show that a flight of six steps descended into the lead-lined tank. In the rubble close by the excavators found the base of a pier with attached pilasters identical in style to the piers in the main baths. Clearly, therefore, the bath and presumably the establishment to which it belonged was

156

of some quality and importance. In fact there can be little doubt that the remains recorded by Irvine are part of another public bathing establishment, for the quality of the work is much too elaborate for a suite of baths attached to a private residence.

It is probably that the establishment was in some way dedicated to a deity or deities, but of the religious aspects of the building we are ignorant except for several altars from the neighbourhood. Two were recovered when the Hot Bath spring was being cleared out in 1774–6. The first, found in 1774, was dedicated to Sulis Minerva by Sulinus, son of Maturus. The second, recovered two years later, is a dedication to Diana. Another altar was found nearby in 1825 during building work connected with the United Hospital. The deity for whom it was set up is unknown but the suppliant is recorded as 'son of Novantius' who erected the altar on behalf of himself and his family. Together the three inscriptions imply that the Roman Hot Bath spring possessed strong religious connections – a point further emphasized by a large number of coins found in the spring in the eighteenth century.

The Cross Bath

The spring now occupied by the Cross Bath also seems to have been used in the Roman period, but there is no evidence of elaborate building. Quite possibly it was enclosed in some simple manner and fitted out for viewing and perhaps worship. The first Roman discovery was made in 1809 when the cistern was cleared out: from a depth of 4m, workmen recovered an altar dedicated to Sulis Minerva and the Divine Household of the Emperor by a soldier, Gaius Curiatius Saturninus. An even more interesting find was made in 1885 while Davis was having the cistern cleared again. This time, from a depth of 6m, a carved block was brought up, depicting scenes from the Aesculapius legend (fig. 98), a very appropriate fitting for a curative spring since Aesculapius was a deity associated with healing. At the same time, an uninscribed altar and the 'walls of the Roman well' were found, but there is a tantalizing lack of further detail.

The 'Religious Place'

Somewhere on the west side of Stall Street, we are told, at its 'lower end', building works in 1753 brought to light three Roman inscriptions. By far the most interesting is an inscription put up by a

98 The clearing out of the Cross Bath spring from time to time has produced several Roman objects of which the most interesting is a block of stone carved with three scenes: one showing a naked woman standing by a reclining male, another showing a quadruped walking beneath a tree, the third a snake curled round a tree. The scenes are thought to represent the Aesculapius legend. Aesculapius is, appropriately, a god of healing. Height 1.3m.

centurion, Gaius Severius Emeritus, for the Divinity of the Emperor at 'This Holy Place, wrecked by insolent hands and cleaned afresh'. The other inscriptions are dedications to the Suleviae and to Loucetius Mars and Nemetona, deities with a distinctly Celtic-fringe flavour.

Since it is very unlikely that the inscriptions were used again in a later building, their presence here may be taken as a reasonable indication of the existence near by of a temple or some other sacred feature. Again, nothing is known of the exact position of the find or of its associated structures, if any, though it is possible that 'lower end of Stall Street' implies the north end rather than the south in which case the inscriptions could have come from the temple precinct.

Roman building in Abbeygate Street (figures 99 and 100)

In contrast to the hasty and ill-recorded discoveries of the eighteenth and nineteenth centuries, it has been possible to carry out several small excavations within the town at a reasonably leisurely pace, in an attempt to trace the occupation of selected areas from the time the site was first inhabited until the construction of cellars during the eighteenth century. One of these sites lay on the north side of Abbeygate Street, beneath two houses, Nos 4 and 5, which had been demolished down to their cellar walls, the demolition rubble fortunately

99 Roman buildings in Abbeygate Street.

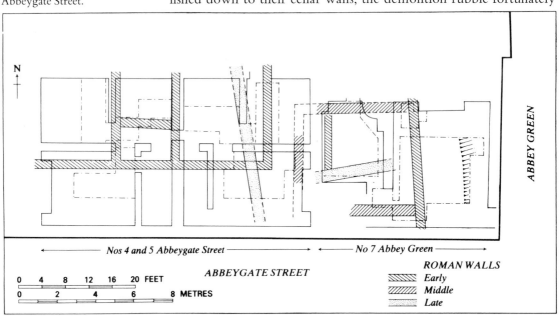

Nos 4 and 5 Abbeygate Street — No 7 Abbey Green

ABBEY GREEN

ABBEYGATE STREET

0 4 8 12 16 20 FEET

0 2 4 6 8 METRES

ROMAN WALLS
Early
Middle
Late

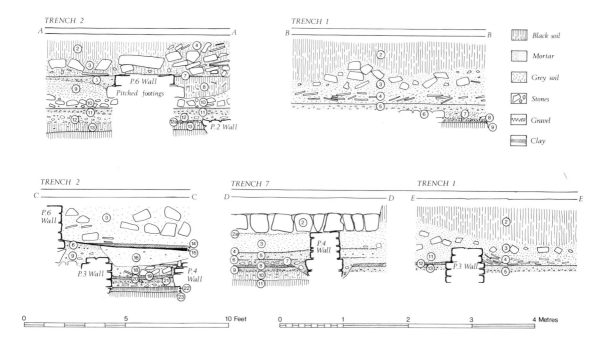

100 Sections through Roman buildings in Abbeygate Street.

being removed. Although the upstanding walls hindered excavation, it was possible to examine a large part of the site throughout the winter of 1964–5 and again in 1971, to build up a detailed picture of the development of this part of the town.

At the beginning of the Roman period and throughout the first and second centuries the site was covered with a layer of black organic mud a little over 30cms thick. A certain amount of rubbish accumulated but there appears to have been little attempt at consolidation or building until the beginning of the third century, when tips of rubble were trampled down to form a hard standing and at least one wall was built. Evidence of lead working in the form of lead offcuts and ceramic tuyères were found at this period. It was not until the late third century that any large-scale construction work was carried out, but then a fairly substantial masonry house, built of neatly coursed lias limestone masonry, was put up. Three of its rooms, floored simply with gravel and mortar, projected into the

161

area excavated, but at this date there was no evidence of particular comfort or elegance. Later, however, during the fourth century, one of the rooms was provided with central heating, by means of a channelled hypocaust and another room was for some reason divided into two. The walls were painted in green, red and white, with red predominating: sometimes areas of red paint were enlivened with frame lines painted as white bands 3mm thick and a few fragments of ochre paint splashed with red show that one of the rooms was painted to represent inlaid marble. Clearly, by this stage, if not before, the building was fitted out in some style. Part of a separate house with a mortar floor and painted walls was found to the east. It too underwent modification at a later date and was partially rebuilt.

Late in the fourth century the houses collapsed. First the roof of blue pennant slabs slid off onto the mortar-floored yard to the south, taking with it the ridge blocks. No attempt was made to salvage usable building stone; instead the shell of the building was left standing, the plaster rendering gradually flaking off the walls and eventually the walls themselves falling in, or being deliberately levelled. The western part of the site now reverted to an open area over which a thick black turf-line accumulated while a completely new building was erected over the eastern part, aligned askew to the third-century building. When the destruction took place cannot be precisely defined, but as the original alterations did not take place until during the fourth century it is unlikely that the building was abandoned much before the early years of the fifth. This makes the building which followed it very late indeed, probably sub-Roman. If it was not actually built after A.D. 410, it must surely have continued in use for some considerable time afterwards for inside a sequence of occupation levels was discovered. First a small oven was built in a hole cut into the mortar floor, and only after a thick layer of ash had accumulated around it was a new floor of clay laid. How long all this lasted is completely unknown, but before the building was finally abandoned the severed head of a young woman was flung into the oven – suggesting perhaps a decline in civilized standards of living. There can be very little doubt, therefore, that the occupation of this site continued long after the official abandonment of the British province in A.D. 410. We may well be looking at Bath during the uneasy period at the end of the fifth century.

Citizen House (figure 101)

A small plot of derelict land in the western part of the walled area was eagerly seized upon during the first campaign of excavations and in 1964 several trial trenches were dug showing just how prolific of Roman structures the site was. In consequence when, in 1970, the intention to rebuild on the site was announced, a more extended programme of work was put in hand.

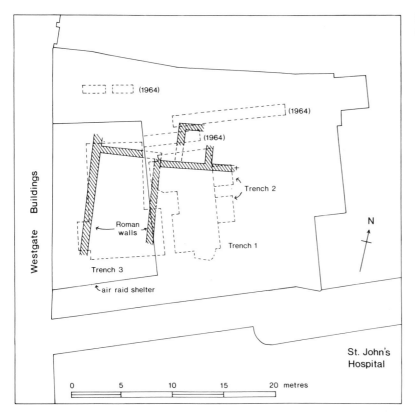

101 Roman buildings on the site of Citizen House.

163

The sequence of occupation spanned the Roman period beginning with timber-built houses in the late first century but quickly developing with masonry houses in the early second century. In both phases the buildings had plastered walls which were attractively painted, while the later masonry building could boast glazed windows. In the second half of the second century the site was cleared and a new masonry building erected. Its outer walls were masonry but the internal partitions were of plastered timber stud work based on dwarf masonry sills. The building was extended and refloored on several occasions throughout the third and fourth centuries during which time it seems to have served as a workshop of some kind. At one stage two small bowl furnaces were in use for forging iron using Somerset coal as the fuel. Eventually in the latter part of the fourth century the building was abandoned and fell into disrepair, a thick layer of soil developing above it.

Although the main sequence of structure could be worked out in some detail the plan recovered was very scrappy because this area had become back gardens in Saxon and mediaeval times and was densely pocked with cesspits and rubbish pits of the ninth to thirteenth centuries. After so much pit digging activity comparatively little of the Roman stratigraphy was left intact!

Nos 30–31 Stall Street (figure 102)

Since both Abbeygate Street and the Citizen House site were under no immediate threat of redevelopment, excavation could be carried out slowly and with care. Not so with the site of two shops in Stall Street, which were demolished and rebuilt as part of the same efficiently organized operation. Apart from a single trial trench cut in a cellar before the rebuilding began, archaeological work had to be restricted to recording and salvaging whilst the new building was being erected: the results are accordingly less detailed than they would have been had the work progressed more slowly under strict archaeological control. Nevertheless, the main sequence of occupation was determined. At a depth of 4m below street-level the original

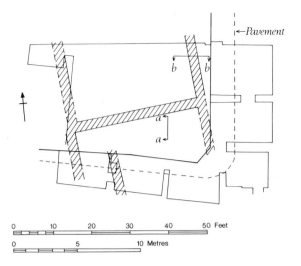

←*Pavement*

b   *b*

a

a

0   10   20   30   40   50 Feet

0   5   10 Metres

102 Roman building beneath
30–31 Stall Street.

black organic turf-line was found overlaid by a series of floors belonging to timber-framed Roman buildings, but no details of their plans
could be recovered. The destruction of one of the buildings was
marked by a thick layer of fine, brown, sandy clay interspersed with
paper-thin patches of paint, which is all that now remains of a painted
wattle and daub wall after it had collapsed and its timber framework
had rotted. From the stratified pottery recovered from these levels
it seems that the buildings date from the late first or early second
century.

Late in the second century or early in the third the site was
levelled with rubble and a massive Roman masonry building was
erected, of which only a small part lay within the development area.
No indication of its size and function has yet been discovered but
its central position and massive construction suggest that it is a building of some importance.

Abbey Green (figure 103)

Not all archaeological finds in Bath in recent years have been made
as the result of planned archaeological excavation. A good example
of a chance find was made when the proprietor of the Crystal Palace

165

103 Roman mosaic found beneath the Crystal Palace public house in Abbey Green.

public house was digging to modify one of his cellars and almost immediately came upon a fragment of a fine mosaic pavement. Only part was exposed but the rest is probably well preserved beneath the yard of the pub. Stylistically the floor would appear to be of second-century date. Later the mosaic was covered by a mortar floor containing pottery of the third or fourth century. A small trial trench dug in the cellar of the house immediately to the north showed that the house with the mosaic was preceded by a thick deposit of occupation debris indicating intense activity in this part of the town.

166

Other Roman buildings from the centre of the settlement

In addition to the more important sites recorded above, a number of other fragments of buildings have come to light since the beginning of the eighteenth century, most of them ill-recorded. But as they provide some idea of the structure and elaboration of the settlement, a brief description of the more substantial remains must be given.

Irvine's rescue work on the site of the United Hospital has already been mentioned in relation to the Roman bathing establishment which he discovered, but the site was a large one and over much of the eastern area a substantial part of what appears to be

104 Drawing of a mosaic found on the site of the Royal United Hospital.

167

105 The first Roman building to be recorded in detail was a house exposed early in the eighteenth century by the architect John Wood during the building of the Mineral Water Hospital. Wood's plan is reproduced here.

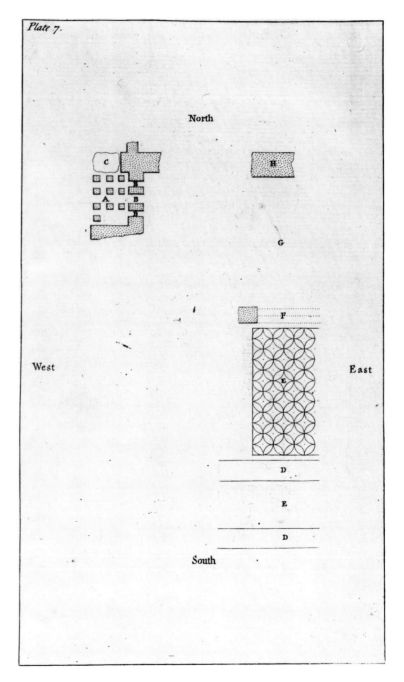

a town-house was recovered (fig. 95). Altogether, about seven rooms were exposed, one of which contained a pillared hypocaust supporting a mosaic 3.2m square depicting a central rosette enclosed within a semi-geometric border (fig. 104). Irvine believed that a 3m wide road ran along the west side of the building towards the temple precinct.

Part of another large house was found in 1738 while the southeast part of the Mineral Water Hospital was being built. Fortunately John Wood, the architect, was on the spot and recorded the Roman features with reasonable accuracy (fig. 105). There were several rooms all belonging to one building. One contained a pillared hypocaust linked by through-vents to another heated room next door. Close by were two mosaics. One belonged to a corridor 1.8m wide, the other, 5.5m across, was evidently from a room of some import-

106 Mosaic found in the nineteenth century on the site of the Mineral Water Hospital; still preserved in position.

169

ance: it was a fine mosaic decorated with intertwined circles. In the north wall a wide doorway, reached by two steps, led up to another room or courtyard paved with slabs. Clearly the house to which these fragments belonged was of some elaboration.

Another tessellated floor was found near by when further building work was carried out in 1859. All that now survives is a fragment of blue and white Greek key design exposed in the basement of the hospital (fig. 106), but the contemporary records suggests the existence of a substantial house with floors of concrete and hypocausts. It was from this site that part of a marble inscription mentioning Tiberius Claudius Sollemnis was found.

107 Mosaic exposed in Bridewell Lane; now destroyed.

Some way to the south, in Bridewell Lane, yet another extension to the Mineral Water Hospital in 1884 exposed part of a further building running beneath the road. Two mosaics were found, the better of which was ornamented with octagonal panels (fig. 107) containing rosettes rather similar to the rosette in the centre of Irvine's mosaic below the United Hospital. Yet another mosaic was found on the corner of Bridewell Lane and Westgate Street in 1814. The Reverend Scarth says 'it was not of superior elegance in design or workmanship'

108 Mosaic from the Bluecoat School now preserved in the Roman Baths Museum.

171

and it appears that it was soon broken up. A much finer floor was found in the north-east corner of the settlement when alterations were made to the Bluecoat School in 1859. It depicts a freely-drawn scene of fabulous sea-beasts in red, blue and brown against a plain white background (fig. 108). The fragment was lifted and is now exhibited in the Roman Baths Museum. Finally, another semi-geometric mosaic was found south of the Abbeygate Street building when Weymouth House School was being reconstructed in 1897. This, too, has been lifted and is now on view in the museum.

There are, of course, large numbers of other objects and fragmentary structures from the town but these are either of little general significance or are badly recorded and located. The above summary does, however, show that the central part of the settlement possessed buildings of some quality. At least eleven are known and there must be others, but whether they were private houses, guest houses or the houses of the staff of the temple and baths we are unlikely ever to know.

The town defences (figures 109 and 110)

Having discussed the buildings within the nucleus of the Roman settlement, it is necessary to turn to the difficult problem of the town defences. There is, of course, no doubt that the town was enclosed within a city wall from mediaeval times until the eighteenth century, when the wall began to be removed to make way for the expanding town. The question is: When was the wall built? The accounts of early excavations across the line give little idea. In 1795, Governor Pownall records 'a Roman wall [4.6m] thick built of a rubble and concrete core faced with large stone blocks' exposed at the south end of Old Bond Street. In 1803 building work close to the Northgate uncovered a wall of massive blocks including much re-used Roman architectural material, and later still, in 1865, Irvine recorded an exposure of the south wall 1.7m thick, opposite the end of Hot Bath Street. None of these discoveries, however, gives any indication of the initial construction date of the defences.

One of the first tasks to confront the newly-formed Bath Excavation Committee in 1963 was the excavation of an area in Upper Borough Walls about to be redeveloped by Messrs Harveys Ltd. The site, which lay along the back of the north wall, provided an admirable opportunity for excavation geared to examine the problems of the northern defences of the town. Without waiting for the demolition of the existing building, occupied by the wine-merchants Cater, Stoffel and Fortts, excavation began amidst the well-stocked wine vaults. Immediately it became apparent that the city wall lay somewhere to the north of the cellars beneath the building, but fortunately it was found that the road, Upper Borough Walls, was built over cellars which communicated directly with the basements of the buildings on both sides. Therefore by working north from Cater, Stoffel and Fortts and south from the buildings on the opposite side of the road, it was possible to obtain an almost complete section through the defensive works (fig. 109).

Several interesting facts emerged. To begin with, it appears that the north side of the town was defended by a rampart of gravel and clay, more than 2m high and 9.1m wide, presumably fronted by a ditch or ditches. A careful examination of material from within the structure of the bank showed that the latest pottery dated to the later years of the second century, whilst from the layers of occupation rubbish which had accumulated later over the tail of the rampart quantities of third- and fourth-century pottery were recovered. Although the evidence is far from conclusive, it tends to suggest that the rampart should be dated broadly to the late second or early third centuries. Attention then switched to the north side of the road where, in two small and extremely awkwardly placed trenches in the less congenial cellars of the Accident Prevention Office, a mass of rubble representing the destroyed and robbed remains of the town wall was sectioned, together with part of its rubble and clay footing dug through early Roman levels. Clearly the point of greatest interest was at the junction between the Roman rampart and the wall. By mere chance, as the drawing (fig. 109) will show, the crucial levels had been thoroughly destroyed by the nineteenth-century spine wall

109 Sections through the city defences at Upper Borough Walls.

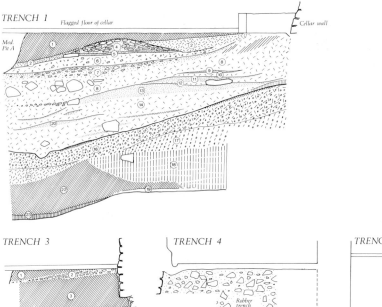

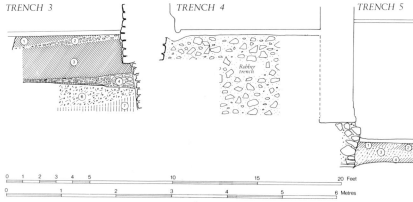

Diagrammatic section of city defences across upper borough walls 1964

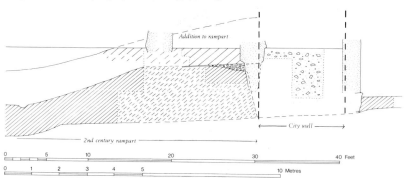

110 The outer face of the city wall, seen here behind the Fernley Hotel, is built of neat, coursed masonry typical of Roman work, but no positive dating evidence has been found to show that the wall is Roman. (Scale in feet.)

which supported the modern road. But even so, all was not lost, for the trench exposed the top of the early rampart, upon which a thin layer of turf had begun to accumulate, sealed by a thick mass of fresh stone chippings. Above this, masses of clay had been thrown down to heighten the rampart. A *possible* explanation of these observations is that the layer of chippings was deposited when the town wall was inserted into the front of the rampart. Since only a very thin turf-line had formed, the deposition of the chippings cannot have taken place very long after the original construction of the rampart. If therefore the chippings belong to the construction of a wall, the wall is likely to be third century or later. Everything hangs on the 'if'. In favour of this interpretation it may be said that late second-century ramparts with third-century walls inserted tend to be a frequently repeated pattern elsewhere in Roman Britain. Bath would seem to echo the norm.

Another opportunity to examine the northern defences came in 1980 when the entire insula between Upper Borough Walls and New Bond Street came up for development. Trial trenching showed that the wall had been fronted by a berm before the edge of a wide flat-bottomed ditch was encountered. This kind of arrangement is quite common among fourth-century defensive circuits and might suggest that the walls of Bath are late Roman in origin.

The question raised by the northern defences clearly demanded the digging of more rampart sections elsewhere around the town, but unfortunately there is at present not a single square metre of available land in the right position. Eighteenth-century builders have covered the defences either with roads or with buildings of merit, whose well-being is closely guarded by the Preservationists. Nevertheless, a considerable section of the outer face of the city wall still survives along the south-east side of the town and an examination of the structure at several points along its line, particularly after the clearance of accumulated rubbish from in front of it, strongly suggests that the work is Roman to a considerable height (fig. 110). The neat coursing and the evenness of size of the blocks give the wall a striking resemblance to good Roman work, but again, until excavation is possible through the layers behind the wall, final answers will not be forthcoming. We are forced, therefore, to the rather unsatisfactory conclusion that while all the existing evidence points to a Roman origin for the town wall at Bath, proof is still lacking.

The town wall now encloses an area of a little under 10 hectares, about a quarter the size of the normal Romano-British cantonal capital. Whatever may be thought of the status of the walled area of Roman Bath it is hardly surprising that the occupied area extended beyond the wall and straggled along the road leading north from the Northgate, in the form of what appears to be a ribbon development. Further areas of occupation have been found across the river at Bathwick.

Our knowledge of the suburb is very patchy, but quantities of occupation material of the second century have been recovered from time to time in the Walcot area, Old Orchard Lane, Guinea Lane and the Paragon, leaving little doubt that these areas were intensively inhabited. Occasionally fragments of buildings have turned up. In 1902, just north of Old Orchard Lane on the east side of Walcot Street, five pier bases, each 1.7m apart, were seen, together with what appears to be part of a hypocaust. Earlier, in 1815, a coarse mosaic was found during the construction of Walcot Brewery, and flue tiles found in a sewer trench in Guinea Lane in 1854–5 suggest the site of yet another building. Other Roman structures include a drain and area of pavement found when a sewer was being laid close to the Northgate, 12m south of St Michael's Church in 1913.

Not far from the church, to the east, the building of the Beaufort Hotel and multi-storey car park in 1971 exposed a Roman pit dug down into the impermeable blue lias clay. The contents had remained waterlogged since Roman times and preserved a magnificent collection of Roman shoes, together with leather offcuts and small iron tools, suggestive of the existence nearby of a cobbler's shop. The pottery from the pit is of late second-century date. Together with the iron-working debris at Citizen House and the traces of a plumber's workshop at Abbeygate Street a picture of the artisans of Roman Bath is beginning to emerge.

Individually the discoveries are insignificant but together they point to a substantial built-up area spreading out from the nucleus of the town along the relatively level strip of land skirting the River Avon. While scattered remains have also turned up south-west and east of the town, they are by no means as dense as the northern settlement.

Summary of the settlement and its development (figure 111)

In the present state of knowledge, any general survey of Roman Bath raises more questions that it provides answers: Bath is a peculiar town, in size much smaller than typical Roman market towns, in

111 Distribution maps of Bath showing where samian pottery of closely datable type has been found indicating the spread of the occupied area at different times.

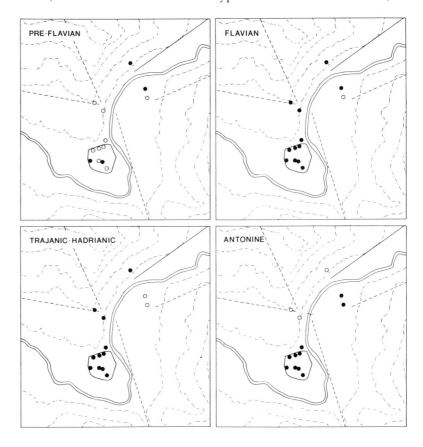

178

elaboration much greater. Its position, at the crossing point of the Fosseway and the River Avon, would have endowed it with a certain military significance in the middle years of the first century when, for a short time, the Fosse formed part of the frontier defences of the newly-won province. The road would have been provided with a chain of forts placed at strategic intervals. One of these may well have occupied the gravel terrace on the Bathwick side of the river where early samian pottery of pre-Flavian date has been found (fig. 111). A fort in this position would have been admirably situated to guard the strategic river-crossing upon which all the major roads appear to converge. No physical trace of it has yet been found but the early military tombstones are additional evidence of the fort's existence and it can only be a matter of time before its position is located.

The springs gushing out of the ground below the 30m terrace seem to have been developed at an early stage, during the latter half of the first century. The Great Baths were built, the first stage of the temple was probably laid out, together perhaps with the adjacent court, and there must have been many subsidiary buildings such as hotels and rest-houses; in fact all the facilities of a successful spa. That the place was a success is shown by the inscriptions left by visitors, who by the beginning of the second century were travelling to Bath from all over the Roman world. At this stage it seems that apart from the principal buildings much of the later walled area was under-developed land, probably without a systematically laid out street grid – in fact little more than a series of buildings and precincts centred on the springs and linked perhaps by pathways. The main settlement area of the second century seems to have remained on the relatively level, well-drained gravel to the north along the line of the Fosseway and across the river in the area of Bathwick.

In the late second and early third centuries the public buildings were probably enclosed first with a rampart and ditch and later, in the fourth century, with a stone wall. From then onwards houses were built within the enclosure, on previously open ground, packed tightly between existing buildings. It may be that the northern settlement area was gradually abandoned as people migrated into the walled area, and Roman Bath began to take on the appearance of a more typical Romano-British town.

Two reasons have been mentioned for the early growth of the settlement: the military significance of the river-crossing and the tourist value of the hot springs. Once it had begun to develop, the economic significance of the site would soon have become apparent.

112 The Bath district in the Roman period.

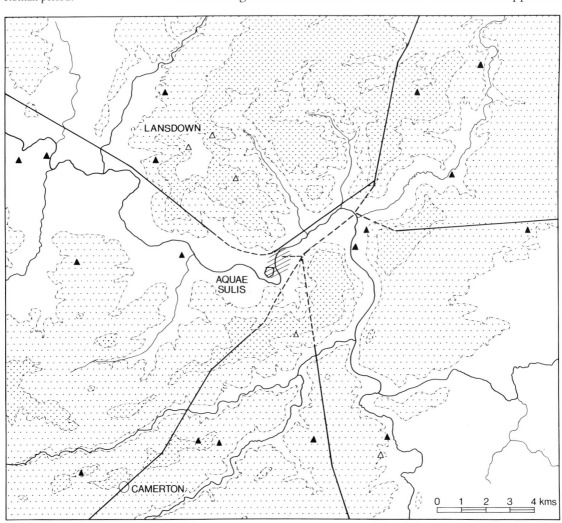

Bath was conveniently sited on a road junction where roads from London, Poole Harbour and Sea Mills (a port close to the mouth of Avon), converged on the Fosseway, which linked the West Country and the Midlands (fig. 112). It also lay in the centre of a rich production area for corn, wool, stone and pewter. Whatever its origins, it cannot have failed to have developed as an important market centre, particularly in the fourth century, by which time the surrounding countryside was densely packed with the villa estates of rich landowners – more than twenty-eight villas are known within a twenty-four-kilometre radius of the town. There is nothing unusual in a religious centre being associated with marketing activities – the combination occurs frequently in the Roman world. Indeed, it is not at all unlike the fairs of mediaeval England, which were always associated with the celebration of Saints' days.

One remaining problem is the administrative status of Bath. Aquae Sulis is listed, along with Winchester, as one of the towns in the administrative territory of the Belgae. While there can be no doubt that Winchester was the principal centre, a strong probability remains that Bath served as a seat of regional government for the western part of the territory – it is, after all, 80km from Winchester and a good 48km from the nearest large towns. No area of this size and economic importance would have been left without an administrative centre.

7

THE PEOPLE OF ROMAN BATH

Over the years casual excavations in Bath have yielded an amazing haul of Roman inscriptions of various kinds: more than forty are now known and there must be many more still to be found. Altogether they provide a unique insight into the composition of the community, mentioning no less than thirty-three different people. Not all sections of the community are represented however, for the poorer people could hardly afford to erect altars to the gods, nor could their families find the money to pay for tombstones for them when they died; but as the survey will show, artisans and retired soldiers were certainly wealthy enough to record themselves for posterity, along with the more high-ranking members of the community. To this group of inscriptions we should add the pewter curses found in the sacred spring. Together they list scores of individuals by name, many of whom would have come from the poorer classes.

To begin with the residents of social distinction, we know of only one priest from the Temple of Sulis, Gaius Calpurnius Receptus, who died at the age of seventy-five and was buried in what is now Sydney Gardens. His tombstone (fig. 113e), a simple affair carved piously in the form of an altar, was put up by his wife, Calpurnia

Trifosa, who had originally been his slave, but to whom he had at some stage granted freedom – presumably before the marriage. The freeing of slaves is recorded a second time in Bath on two altars found within the temple precinct, erected for the same man, Marcus Aufidius Maximus, a retired centurion of the Sixth Legion Victrix, one by Aufidius Eutuches, the other by Marcus Aufidius Lemnus (fig. 120a). Both men are referred to as 'his freedman', suggesting perhaps an act of thanks for the master by two of his newly-freed slaves.

Another of the temple employees was Lucius Marcius Memor, whose inscribed statue base has already been mentioned (fig. 29). As a *haruspex* he would have been a member of an elite class of augurers who officiated in the principal temples of the Empire, foretelling the future through their closely-guarded knowledge of omens. One wonders whether he would have been a resident in Bath, working full-time in the temple, or simply a visitor passing through. Two other dignitaries connected with the temple have already been referred to: Claudius Ligur and Gaius Protacius, who were responsible for the restoration and repainting of a monument or building belonging to the temple. Both were probably public-minded citizens willing to show their devotion to the gods, and incidentally to their fellows, by making a donation in aid of good works.

Bath must have had something of a cosmopolitan air about it in the Roman period, not unlike the town today at the height of the holiday season. There were the retired soldiers living in and around the town, soldiers on leave visiting the spring, and a constant stream of tourists from Britain and abroad, all drawn to the spa by stories of the curative properties of the waters. Some of the soldiers, like the cavalryman Lucius Vitellius Tancinus (fig. 114), a Spaniard from Caurium serving with the *ala Vettonum*, who died at the age of forty-six after twenty-six years of service, may possibly have been stationed at the supposed fort at Bath. The same may also be true of Marcus Valerius Latinus and Antigonus, both soldiers of the Twentieth Legion. Neither of the last two tombstones bears the words *Valeria Victrix* after the title of the legion, a fact which suggests that the tombs were erected at an early date in the first century, before the legion had won the honours, at which time the two soldiers may well have been on active service. Whatever may have been the position of these three, other soldiers recorded from the town were visitors or retired veterans choosing the enervating atmosphere of Bath

(a)

(b)

113 Tombstones and other inscriptions from Bath:

(a) Tombstone of the little girl Mercatilla, who died when only eighteen months. Height 61cm.

(b) Tombstone of Julius Vitalis, armourer of the Twentieth Legion, erected by members of the craft guild to which he belonged. Height 1.85m.

in which to spend their declining years. Some of the soldiers died at an unnaturally early age, people such as Julius Vitalis (fig. 113*b*), an armourer of the Twentieth Legion recruited in Gallia Belgica, who died after only nine years' service, aged twenty-nine; and Gaius Murrius Modestus, of the Second Adiutrix Legion, from Forum Julii,

(c)

113 (c) Tombstone of Rusonia Aventina, a visitor from Metz. Width 94cm.

in southern France, who died aged twenty-five. They must have been ailing from disease or wounds when they visited Bath, never to return to their legions. Vitalis belonged to a craft guild, equivalent now to a Friendly Society. When he died his colleagues paid for his cremation and tombstone, carefully recording on it 'with funeral at the cost of the Guild of Armourers'. Even a young soldier could be assured of a decent burial if he belonged to a guild.

Other soldiers settled in Bath after demobilization. Marcius Aufidius Maximus, the centurion of the Sixth Legion, has already been mentioned in relation to the slaves he freed. By this time he was probably a prosperous local figure living in comfortable retirement. Another soldier, unnamed, probably settled in the north suburbs of the town, where he lost his bronze diploma issued to all soldiers on their retirement. He had served in a cavalry regiment, the *ala I Gallorum Proculeiana*, early in the second century and like all time-expired veterans was granted the right of citizenship after

185

(d)

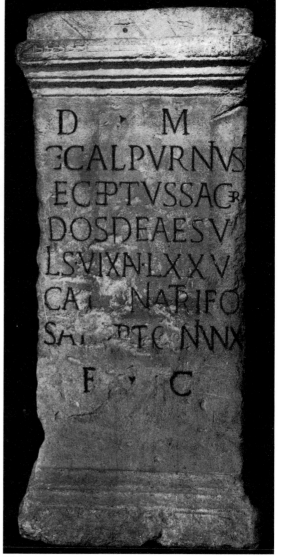

113 (d)   The son of Novantius set this up as the result of a vision. Height 46cm.

    (e)   Tombstone of the old priest Gaius Calpurnius Receptus, erected by his wife, once his slave. Height 1.35m.

(e)

twenty-five years' service. As a man in his mid-forties, he and possibly his family, chose Bath as a congenial town in which to begin his new life, perhaps as a craftsman, a farmer or a merchant. There must have been many more like him living and working in the surrounding countryside. Was Gaius Curiatius Saturninus, a centurion of the Second Augustan Legion, also a retired soldier, or was he still on active service with his legion stationed at Caerleon just across the Bristol Channel? We know of him because of the altar he set up at the Cross Bath spring to Sulis Minerva and to the deities of the Emperors either in repayment for a request which the goddess had answered, or in anticipation of a satisfactory response.

Less certainty attaches to the standing of the centurion Gaius Severius Emeritus, who dedicated an altar (fig. 120*b*) recording his act of piety in cleansing afresh 'this holy spot wrecked by insolent hands'. He styles himself 'centurion in charge of this region', implying that he may have been a military administrator, perhaps responsible for a near-by Imperial estate. The Roman settlement at Combe Down, near Bath, has produced an inscription recording a *principia* which is thought to refer to the headquarters of local procuratorial administration, and a lead seal found on the same site, stamped *p(rovinciae) Br(itanniae) S(uperioris)* shows that official parcels were passing through. It may be that Emeritus ran the establishment for a while. It is interesting to question whose 'insolent hands' wrecked the holy place with which Emeritus was concerned. Could it perhaps have been the Christians who, in the new-found power of the official recognition afforded to them in the early fourth century, would have found much to react against in the great pagan centre of Bath? There must have been many, like Emeritus, ready to restore the old pagan order when the wave of iconoclasm had passed.

Bath lay at the centre of a rich stone-producing area, and its fine-grained cream coloured oolitic limestone soon became well known and widely used throughout the province. We know of two masons who visited the spa: Priscus, son of Toutius (fig. 133*f*) and Sulinus, son of Brucetius (fig. 120*c*), both recorded on inscribed dedicatory altars. The Priscus inscription was found close to the baths and is dedicated to Sulis, whilst the offering of Sulinus, found at the 'holy place' at the lower end of Stall Street, was dedicated to a collection of local deities, the Suleviae. Priscus was a foreign visitor from the tribe of the Carnutes centred on modern Chartres. As a *lapidarius* (stone worker) he must have taken a professional interest in the local stone quarries, but even if he was on a business trip he would presumably have indulged in the pleasures that Bath had to offer. Sulinus, who styles himself a sculptor, poses more interesting problems because the same man is recorded on an altar, again dedicated to the Suleviae, discovered at Cirencester, 45km north of Bath. The inscription was found at Ashcroft towards the west side of the Roman town in 1899, together with eight other sculptured stones, all in a well preserved fresh condition. Two of them depicted the Triad of Deae Matres, the three mother goddesses so popular in north and west Britain; the third was a statuette of a cloaked female, possibly a single mother, whilst the fourth was a base for a similar piece. The other objects included the head of a female, an inscribed altar and two pieces of columns. Exactly how this collection should be interpreted is uncertain. It may be the remains of a shrine or temple, but the fresh nature of the individual carvings is certainly suggestive of a mason's working yard, as the original excavator thought. If so, it may be the workshop of Sulinus. Did he perhaps visit Bath to buy stone from the local quarries? Some of the pieces from the Cirencester yard are carved from Bath stone, but this of course proves nothing. The facts as we know them are full of fascinating possibilities but they leave the situation wide open.

One other stone worker should be mentioned: the unnamed craftsman who engraved the superb collection of gemstones found within the culvert leading from the spring reservoir. A recent study of the individual intaglios leaves little doubt that all thirty-three gems were engraved by the same school of craftsmen or even perhaps the same man. Someone put them in a bag and flung it into the spring as an offering to the deity. Was it the engraver himself dedicating a sample of his work or did someone else buy them from him? If it was the craftsman, did he work in Bath, gearing his output to the tourist industry, or was he a visitor? These are questions to which we will never know the answers.

The stonemason Priscus from Chartres is a reminder of the great tourist attraction that the spa must have provided. People would have flocked to the town from all over the Roman world. Some erected altars to the gods for their safe journey or their recovery or for some other service, whilst those less favoured by the gods died, only to be commemorated by their tombstones. Several visitors have already been mentioned, but we know of others. Rusonia Aventina, a middle-aged lady of the Mediomatrici (fig. 113c), a tribe centred on Metz,

(f)

113 (f)   Priscus, son of Toutius, a stonemason from Chartres, erected this for the goddess Sulis. Height 53cm.

189

died in Bath at the age of fifty-eight. She was buried in the cemetery to the north of the town by her heir, Lucius Ulpius Sestius. Was he perhaps a relation who had escorted her from home? Did he come across especially for the funeral? Or was he someone the lady had met in Britain? Again, intriguing but unanswerable questions.

Another foreigner, Perigrinus, son of Secundus, a Treveran in origin from the area around modern (Trier (fig. 120a), offered an altar to his two favourite deities, Loucetius Mars and Nemetona. This particular inscription was one of the group found in 1753 at the 'holy place' at the lower end of Stall Street. Most of these were dedicated to gods other than Sulis Minerva, suggesting a temple or shrine unattached to the god's sacred springs, a place where travellers could thank their own patron gods for a safe journey without risk of disrespect to the presiding deity.

It is a great pity that so little survives to enable the social round of the visitor to be reconstructed. Visits to the baths, temple and 'theatre' would naturally have featured prominently and there must have been hotels (*mansiones*) for the comfort of travellers, but of the shops, taverns and other facilities offering amusement and distraction, we are at present ignorant. It is possible, too, that there were dormitories provided for the sick or for those who wished to spend time in solitary meditation, like the building found in the great pagan centre at Lydney on the other side of the Bristol Channel, where Nodens was worshipped. One man, the son of Novantius, had a vision which led him to set up a dedicatory inscription on behalf of himself and his family (fig. 113d). This might have happened whilst he was in the town, but it could equally well be that the gods directed him to go there. There must have been many in this position roaming the precincts of the spa, the devout seeking out the magicians and the soothsayers, the sick visiting doctors and opticians. One doctor, Tiberius Junianus, lost his medicine stamp which eventually turned up 1,500 years later in 1731, when a cellar was constructed near the Abbey Yard. Bath would have been a happy hunting-ground for skilled medical practitioners, quacks and charlatans alike; tourists on holiday are always easy prey.

In spite of the watchful eye of the goddess and the salubrious atmosphere, the death rate here, as elsewhere in the empire, was high, and people died young. One tombstone, seen by Leland built into the town wall west of the Northgate, records the death of a little girl, Successa Petronia. It was put up by her parents, Vettius Romulus and Victoria Sabina, and mentions that she lived to three years four months and nine days. Another girl, the foster-daughter of Magnius, called Mercatilla, was only eighteen months old when she died (fig. 113*a*). Her tombstone, found in 1809 near the Northgate, probably came from the cemetery which grew up along the Fosse-way. In the same cemetery lay another young woman whose funerary inscription simply records: 'Vibia Jucunda, aged thirty, lies buried here.' But not everyone died in youth: one old town councillor (*decurion*) from the colonia in Gloucester lived to the ripe old age of eighty.

Of the other *dramatis personae* of Roman Bath who remain to be mentioned, there is Tiberius Claudius Sollemnis, recorded for posterity on a slab of white Italian marble, his name linked to that of Sulis, suggesting perhaps that he endowed a rich monument to the goddess. An altar put up by another of the deity's devotees, Quintus Pompeius Anicetus, was found in York Street; and finally yet another altar, erected by Sulinus son of Maturus, was dedicated to the same deity, this time at the Hot Bath spring. The survey of those who inhabited or visited the spring in the Roman period has been long, but it demonstrates how fortunate the archaeologists of Bath are to have so full a record, unparalleled in Britain outside the military north. The rows of dull-looking inscriptions which now fill the Roman Baths Museum can very easily be turned into a complex picture of a vigorous Roman community.

The pewter curses thrown into the spring by aggrieved inhabitants of Bath have been discussed, in so far as they reflect on religious beliefs, in Chapter 2: here we must look briefly at what they have to say about the people. Altogether over a hundred different names are listed and occasionally we are given rare insights into family groups. Curse no. 618, which reminds the goddess of a vow sworn at the spring on 12 April, mentions six people: Uricalus, Docilosa his wife, Docilis and Docilina his son and daughter, and his brother Decentinus with his wife Alogiosa. It is interesting to see that the two brothers Uricalus and Decentinus have respectively a Celtic and a Latin name, suggesting that, in this case, their father did not recognize the difference as socially significant. But that there may, indeed, have been a status difference between Celtic and Latin names is hinted at by two more curses nos. 206 and 612. No. 206 lists eleven names among the possible miscreants, two women: Severa and Surilla; and nine men: Dracontius, Spectatus, Innocentius, Senicio, Candidianus, Simplicius, Belator, Austus and Carinianus. We are given no further details of them but two of the names, Belator and Surilla, are both Celtic while the rest are Latin. No. 612 gives us eleven names and some details about them: Roveta, Vitoria and Vindocunus her husband, Cunomolius and Minervina his wife, Cunitius the slave and Senovara his wife, Lavidendus the slave, Mattonius the slave, Catinius the tax collector's thief, and Methianus. Of this list only two, Vitoria and Minervina, have Latin names, the rest are Celtic. In this case it looks very much as though we are dealing with a group of lower-class individuals, among them three slaves. Comparing the two curses it is tempting to suggest that the families who preferred to continue using Celtic names may generally have been socially inferior. It is an interesting insight into Romano-Celtic society to be further examined as more curses are translated.

The summary of the epigraphic evidence given in the first part of this chapter gives some hint of the type of life followed by those who lived in, or were dependent upon, the town. A substantial part of the population must have been geared to providing for the tourist traffic: there were those who officiated and served in the temples and baths, the hoteliers and their servants, the doctors and the small traders, but the existence of a specialized tourist industry should not obscure the fact that Bath lay at the centre of a territory rich both agriculturally and in terms of the mineral deposits thereabouts. Some measure of local productivity can be gauged from the density of

Roman villas in the countryside around the town (fig. 112), many of which, judging from their fine mosaic pavements, were the centres of profitable estates. Too little is yet known of the growth of individual villas to allow the economic development of the region to be traced in any detail, but in general terms the luxury villas seem to have reached their exalted status only by the beginning of the fourth century, a pattern which holds good for most parts of Britain. Elsewhere it is often possible to show a gradual rise in the material wealth of the villa owners reflected in the buildings themselves, starting with relatively unostentatious farmhouses in the first and second centuries and developing over the years by the gradual accretion of luxuries such as central heating, mosaic floors and baths. Superficially it would seem that by the fourth century a greater disparity existed in the countryside between the rich and the poor, the rich getting gradually richer while many of the peasants lived in poverty, becoming increasingly more dependent upon the large landowners.

The agrarian wealth of the Bath region was probably based on a mixed economy in which cattle-rearing and sheep farming would have played an important part alongside cereal production. It is impossible, in the present state of knowledge, to assess the nature of chronological or regional changes in the balance. Many of the plateau areas, such as Charmey Down and Bathampton Down, are covered with field systems suggestive of agricultural activity of some intensity; while the steep-sided valleys would have been ideal for sheep grazing, the valley floors providing lush grass for herds of cattle. It has been suggested that elsewhere in the country there was a major change-over to sheep farming by the fourth century, wool becoming more profitable than grain since it was less heavily taxed. Whether this is generally true or not, and the matter is still in dispute, there is no firm evidence from any of the villas of the Bath region to throw light on the matter. The problem can only be resolved by new large-scale excavations of several villas.

The relationship between the villas and the town was close. Whatever the stature of Bath was in the early years of the occupation, there can be little reasonable doubt that by the third century it had

developed an administrative and economic significance equivalent
to that of the typical cantonal capital. It would have been ruled by
a town council (*ordo*) composed of a hundred ex-magistrates (*decuriones*) who had attained certain property qualifications. These men
would have lived in those country villas or town houses which might
reasonably be expected to show some signs of wealth. Within a reasonable commuting distance of the town there are about thirty
known villas of quality, while in the town traces of some eleven
houses are at present recorded, most of which are likely to be private
dwellings. The figures are *minimum* numbers, but they might suggest
that the number of decurions living within the town was about a
quarter of the total, the rest choosing to stay in their country estates.
These calculations are, of course, rough and open to criticism
but it might be significant that, on the much better evidence from
Silchester, Sir Ian Richmond arrived at the same percentages.

There were other sources of wealth in the area besides farming.
The value of Bath stone has already been mentioned. The quarries,
which served most of the principal sites in the south of the province,
would have provided regular work for the local peasants and a substantial income for the leaseholders or owners of the workings. The
very existence of the stone would have encouraged the growth of
schools of craftsmen geared to the production of standard architectural details and blanks for altars and tomb reliefs. One blank altar
was actually found at Bathwick in 1900 with guide-lines scribed on
it ready for inscription. Perhaps it stood in the working yard of a
local mason, waiting to be purchased by a visitor, first to be inscribed
with suitable sentiments and then to be erected in the temple.

While there is no doubt about the economic importance of Bath
stone, less certainty attaches to the exploitation of local coal. That
it was used as a fuel in the neighbourhood is not in question, indeed
we have seen that coal was probably burnt on the altar of Sulis
Minerva, but whether a significant percentage of the population were
engaged in mining or quarrying is at present an open question. Similar doubt attaches to the significance of pennant stone, a blue closely-
laminated sandstone, which attained a widespread popularity as a

roofing and flooring material. The local demand could probably have been easily met by the sporadic working of the quarries.

One of the more important industries of the Bath region was the manufacture of pewter vessels, which reached a peak in the fourth century. Pewter was essentially a cheap local substitute for silver, and when from the middle of the third century the unrest and economic crisis in the empire greatly increased the value of silver out of all proportion, the moderately wealthy, who required exotic-looking tableware, were forced to resort to the use of pewter, an alloy of tin and lead, which to some tastes was not found to be wholly unattractive. Why pewter manufacture should centre on Bath is not immediately apparent. Tin from Cornwall and lead from the Mendips could conveniently be transported along the Fosseway, it is true, but Ilchester is rather more centrally placed in an equally rich area. The answer may, of course, be that pewter working was far more widespread in the west of Britain and that it is by mere chance that the only two manufacturing sites at present known lie within a few miles radius of Bath.

Camerton, 13km south of the town along the Fosseway, provides the best idea of an industrial site (fig. 112). Here excavation has shown the gradual growth of a ribbon development along the main road, comprised of scattered rectangular workshops 20 to 24 m long and about 3m wide, most of them provided with ovens and furnaces of a type suitable for pewter manufacture, as well as for a host of other domestic purposes. In one of the workshops two stone moulds were found, in which the metal would have been cast, one in the form of an oblong dish, the other to make a handle. From elsewhere in the settlement two other pewter plates and a handle were recovered. It would be wrong to suggest that the inhabitants of the village owed their entire livelihood to the manufacture of pewter vessels. Farming activities must have continued to play an important part in everyday life, but the growth of a specialist cottage industry would have helped the peasants to eke out a meagre existence at what must have been a very difficult period for those with little or no land of their own.

114 The tombstones from the cemetery which grew up along the Fosseway leading to the North gate, sometimes depict people. Two reliefs are from military tombstones showing cavalrymen trampling down their enemies. The inscribed stone commemorates Lucius Vitellius Tancinus; the other two reliefs probably show local dignitaries. (Scales approx. $\frac{1}{10}$).

The second of the pewter production sites lies on the high land of Lansdown, about 5km north-west of Bath, where excavations at the beginning of the century exposed a peasant settlement of considerable extent. Quantities of fourth-century coins and pottery suggest that the greatest development came late, but there is good reason to suggest a very early origin for the settlement. Among the finds recovered is a remarkable collection of stone moulds for the production of a range of pewter objects, including dishes, plates, handles for jugs and decorative roundels of various kinds. Here, as at Camerton, there can be little doubt that the pewter industry had grown to be an essential part of the subsistence economy.

Marketing the products would have provided no problem, the craftsmen or their employers needing to undertake only a short journey into Bath to find a ready market among the visitors and merchants. Some may have sold their products in bulk to middlemen for distribution from secondary markets in the other towns of the provinces, others would have disposed of individual pieces or sets to the agents of neighbouring landowners who came into Bath to purchase their day-to-day needs. It may be that one craftsman dedicated part of his stock to the presiding deity and threw it into the sacred spring, where it sank to the bottom, some pieces being washed out into the culvert, to be found by excavators 1,500 years later.

Such, then, are some of the activities in which the inhabitants of Aquae Sulis and its neighbourhood would have been engaged in the Roman period. Indeed, there would have been very little difference between Bath of the fourth century and the town as late as the seventeenth century. In size, population and economic basis there are many points of close similarity.

Having discussed the people and their lives, we must briefly consider them in their death. Large numbers of Roman burials have come to light over the years from the neighbourhood of the town (fig. 115), but practically without exception the discoveries were made accidentally and recording, where any was attempted at all, is inadequate. Nevertheless, it is possible to obtain a general impression of the burial practices of the inhabitants. The earliest burials,

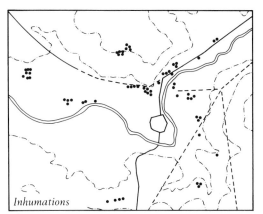

Inhumations

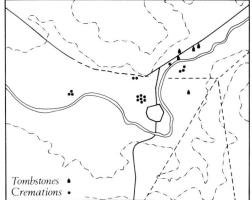

Tombstones ▲
Cremations •

dating to the first and second centuries, were cremations, the bones being placed in urns and buried, often with smaller pots of finer quality containing offerings of food to sustain the spirit on its journey to the other world. The poorer cremations would probably have been marked by a simple wooden or stone marker, whilst the richer burials would have been located by inscribed tombstones of the type we have already considered. The tombstone of Julius Vitalis (fig. 113*b*) the armourer of the Twentieth Legion, for example, was found in 1708 close to two simple cinerary urns, one presumably containing food, the other Vitalis himself. Generally speaking, the richer the occupant the more ostentatious the tomb. Several of the tombs were adorned with sculptures of considerable merit. From the cemetery area at Walcot a colossal head of a woman was recovered, evidently a portrait of a fierce-looking lady wearing her hair in a mass of tight curls in a style fashionable in Rome in the late first century (fig. 116). Presumably the head once adorned her tomb. Another head, of the theatrical mask of Tragedy (fig. 117), must also have come from a tomb. Three tomb reliefs are also known. One, found in 1803 built into the north wall, shows a man wearing a short tunic and a cloak holding a standard in one hand and a scroll in the other (fig. 114). His large purse is dominantly featured, hanging from his belt. A second relief, found at the same time, shows a man with hands folded across his body, probably holding a scroll

115 The cemeteries of Bath.

199

116 Colossal head of a woman whose hair is set in a manner fashionable in Rome in the late first century A.D. Possibly a tomb sculpture. From Walcot.

117 Sculptured theatrical mask: probably a tomb relief. From Walcot.

118 Animal sculptures abound in Bath. They are all lively and accomplished representations possibly made by the same school of craftsmen.

(a)   Lion carrying a young deer across its back. From London Road, Walcot. Height 40cm.

(b)   A boar. From the baths. Height 44cm.

(c)   A lion. Dredged from the River Avon. Height 27cm.

(a)

(b)

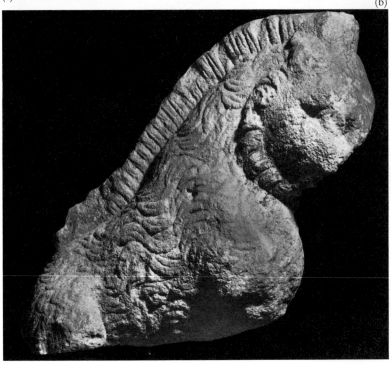

(c)

119 Tomb relief from Bathwick. A hound chases a hare over a tree. Symbolic of the spirit of the departed escaping. Height 53cm.

120

(a) Altar to Loucetius Mars and Nemetona put up by Peregrinus, a native of Trier. Height 76cm.

(b) Altar put up by Severius Emeritus, the centurion in charge of the region. Height 91cm.

(fig. 114); he wears a toga and his hair is brushed forward and cut short. Both depict prominent citizens, men of wealth and status, who indulged in Roman manners and dress, and who might well have been decurions. The third relief, which probably comes from a tomb, was dug up in London Road in Walcot in 1860. Though only a small piece, it shows a brilliant rendering of a lion carrying a deer across its back (fig. 118). It is one of the most accomplished sculptures from Roman Britain.

(a)

(b)

Fragmentary though our knowledge of the funerary monuments of Bath is, the surviving pieces give a reasonably balanced picture of what it was like to travel north from the town along the Fosseway in the second century. It must have been very similar to an elongated Victorian churchyard with its range of simple markers, inscribed headstones and elaborate family vaults.

Several times mention has been made of the fact that fragments

(c) Altar to the Suleviae, erected by the sculptor Sulinus who may have lived and worked in Cirencester. Height 59cm.

(d) Altar to the goddess Sulis erected for Aufidius Maximus by his freedman. Height 1.27m.

(c)

(d)

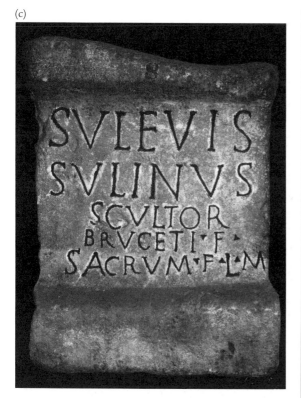

of funerary monuments were built into the city wall. This raises the interesting question of when this was done. Was the early cemetery largely dismantled when the walls were built, possibly in the third century, and the monuments used as rubble, or were the Roman stones used to patch the existing wall in late Saxon or mediaeval times? The use of funerary monuments as ballast in town walls is certainly well attested in Gaul during the third century and some of the bastions of London incorporate re-used stone of this kind, but there is now some doubt as to whether they are fourth century, as originally supposed, or later. Thus while it is an attractive possibility that the old cemetery along the Fosseway was dismantled for use in the construction of the Roman town wall, without further excavation, which is not at the moment possible, the question must remain open.

The changeover from cremation to inhumation took place gradually throughout the third century, providing incidentally a great boost for the local stone industry which was now required to produce large quantities of stone sarcophagi for those who could afford them. The less wealthy were buried in simple wooden coffins while occasionally more expensive lead lining was used, as in the case of the coffin found at Bathwick in 1819. The early records of the discoveries of Roman inhumations give some idea of the rituals involved and the beliefs of the people. Often the dead were provided with coins to pay Charon to ferry the soul across the River Styx; sometimes, for example with one of the Combe Down burials, the coin was placed on the lips of the departed. Generally, grave goods were not common, but dress pins, rings and brooches show that the bodies were clothed, while the discovery of hobnails at the feet implies that often people were buried in their boots. Occasionally more exotic offerings were placed in the graves, as in the burial found near Sydney Buildings which included a bronze box 'which opened with a spring' containing eight bronze coins.

Generally the bodies were laid on their backs in various orientations, but examples are known from the Bath area where the dead were laid face-downwards in their coffins, presumably for some religious reason. Two burials, found at Bathwick Hill in 1861, are of particular interest. Both bodies were placed in stone coffins, one packed in fine white sand, the other in a coarser sand. The first coffin contained a young woman, the second a child of fourteen or fifteen years. This may well be an example of an attempt at preserving the body from decay in the same way that gypsum was used for this purpose in York. Tiny pieces of fabric were said to have been found preserved in the sand, together with particles of a bituminous material which might hint at some form of embalming. The sand was unfortunately not analysed, but fine white sand is sometimes deposited by the spring and it may be that such a deposit was considered to have preservative qualities. These Bathwick Hill burials provide an interesting insight into the aspiration of the inhabitants of the town and their hopes of a happy after-life.

8

THE END OF ROMAN BATH

The end came to different parts of the town at different times. First to suffer were the baths and the temple, which together lay in a slight hollow in the centre of the settlement around the main spring. It seems that throughout the third and fourth centuries the sea-level had been rising and with it the general water table of the inland areas, causing a series of floods of gradually increasing severity. It was to counteract the flooding of the hypocausts that the levels of the basement floors were raised late in the development of the baths, but as time went on even the new floors suffered sporadic submersion and thick layers of grey and black mud were deposited by the flood waters between the *pilae* of the hypocausts. The discovery of these silts raised the question of whether or not it was the spring water that was causing the damage. However, a detailed chemical analysis established beyond doubt that the muds were the result of flood waters from the River Avon backing up along the drains at times when the river was in full spate. The sediment was gradually precipitated from the standing water, which eventually receded leaving the mud to dry. Then the river would again flood and the process would begin once more. Exactly the same problems of flooding still exist today. Though modern river controls are reducing the frequency of flooding, until quite recently each year, often several times a year, the water backed up, leaving strand lines 1.2 to 1.5m above general floor level.

Faced with the problem, there was very little the Roman engineers could do but wait for the water to recede. It must have meant periods of days or even weeks when the establishment would have been out of use. As the economic and political stability of the province began to shake, the impetus, or the financial ability, to clear out the mud and repair the flood damage would have weakened until at one particular point in time it was decided to abandon the establishment altogether. But perhaps this is putting it too strongly – it might be more accurate to say that the decision to re-open the baths failed to be taken. The mud remained and the end had begun.

One of the most glaring omissions of the Victorian excavations was their virtual lack of interest in the mud and soil which choked the Baths. To the excavators it was rubbish to be removed as soon as possible. Irvine attempted to record some archaeological sections, but by the time most of the work was being undertaken he had left Bath and there was no one of his calibre to take over. In consequence there is practically nothing to be said of the processes involved in the gradual destruction of the building. On the other hand the adjacent temple area, much of which escaped Victorian clearance, still retains its overburden of silt and rubble to a depth of 2m.

The excavations of 1965–8 and 1981–3 allowed these fascinating layers to be examined in detail: incorporated in the soil was the entire story of the temple precinct from the moment the last feet walked upon the clean pennant paving in the fourth century until the area became a graveyard in late Saxon and early mediaeval times – 2m of soil representing seven hundred years of neglect and change (fig. 121). For ease of discussion we have divided the late sequence into four periods – periods 5–8 (periods 1–4 being the earlier building phases of the temple, pp. 58–74). During period 5 we see the attempts of the late or sub-Roman population to keep the old building in use but the Roman drainage system had broken down and the

121 The temple precinct during excavation. Beyond the horizontal rod scale the thick layer of soil represents successive floors and mud accumulations reflecting continuous use. The latest is sealed by the collapse of the superstructure.

low-lying area of the inner precinct around the altar seems to have become susceptible to periodic flooding. At any event thick black soil began to accumulate. Periodically the ground surface was consolidated with a tip of rubble or a spread of poor quality concrete but still the waterlogging occurred and more soil and silt accumulated until the deposit had grown to a depth of 60cms. Fortunately some of the pollen of the locally growing plants became incorporated in the mud and because of its semi-waterlogged condition a reasonable sample has survived. Very common were grains of various grasses and the usual garden weeds such as the dandelion family (*Linguli-*

210

florae) together with pollen from cereals and the weeds of cultivation which characterize farmed land, plants such as ribwort plantain. All these probably indicate what was being grown in the general locality rather than the specific spot in the centre of the town. Other plants more related to the actual marsh were the sedges, reedmace and the gentians. Mosses, ferns and bracken were also represented, all typical of marshy conditions which by this time must have lain within and around the buildings. While the waterlogging prevailed in the low-lying parts around the baths and temple, the rest of the town, unaffected by the flooding, continued to be inhabited, its rubbish, including pottery and animal bones, now being tipped into the precinct area.

The last repaving was carried out on a more substantial scale. The portico north of the reservoir and part of the area of the precinct to the north was paved with close-set limestone slabs robbed from standing Roman buildings. The niched quadrangular monument (above, pp. 90–1) was used in this way and so was the fine relief of Diana's hound (fig. 58) but even more interesting was the discovery of one of the blocks of the temple pediment, used upside-down as paving, in the excavation of 1982. It now seems highly likely that the other pediment blocks, found in 1790, had also been used in this way but since their backs were sawn off and discarded at the time of discovery, it is no longer possible to see if they, like the 1982 block, were worn.

The re-use of sculptured monuments as paving raises many interesting questions: was this done deliberately as an act of desecration and if so when and by whom? It was at about this time that the altar was dismantled and its corners pushed over. Together the evidence is suggestive of some conscious process designed to remove the iconography of the pagan religion. One *possible* context for this would be the foundation of the Christian monastic community in Bath by Osric in A.D. 675 when one might have expected the more obvious signs of paganism to have been removed. Sadly we will never know.

The new paving, which marks the last constructional phase of period 5, remained in active use for some while, becoming very worn. All this time the temple buildings were still standing. Then, in period 6, the superstructure of the portico and possibly part of the reservoir enclosure, collapsed, or was pushed over, creating a scree of massive stone blocks mixed up with slabs of concrete and shattered tiles from the vaults (fig. 122). Whether or not the collapse was deliberately contrived, it is clear that the inhabitants raked through the rubble to remove the iron clamps and their lead settings which had once held the structure together leaving the thick layer of rubble to serve as a convenient foundation for subsequent floors. Dating

122 The temple precinct. The tumbled mass of the portico in front of the reservoir enclosure seen here just as it fell in the Saxon period.

212

is difficult but by this time we must be in the eighth or ninth century. Already, in the centre of the precinct where the soil was deeper and less rubbly, a cemetery was beginning to develop marking the beginning of a long period of burial which came to an end in the sixteenth century with the Dissolution.

Whilst we can be specific about the inner precinct, how the entire complex – the baths, spring and temple – fared we can only guess.

After the roofs had fallen in, the old monument must have formed a dramatic and rather sad sight, with its columns, piers and probably its entablatures standing in ruins, projecting gauntly from the engulfing marsh. Towards the centre would have been the bubbling, steaming spring, the waters swirling away from the sources and lapping against fallen and standing masonry alike, leaving a thick crust of bright red iron oxide stain on everything. Away from the source would have been lagoons of still, black water giving way to drier land upon which reeds, bracken and small trees such as willow and alder grew, providing homes for wild fowl like the coot or teal, whose egg was found in the old excavations, and for innumerable wild animals. In fact much of the centre of the town would have reverted to the state in which the Roman engineers found it – except for the incongruous framing of Roman masonry which projected without obvious reason from a predominantly rural scene. The image which constantly springs to mind is of a stage set for a willowy Victorian romance – slightly ominous grey architecture seen against wispy blue-green light. It was into this setting that the early Christian community was injected.

The drama of the ruins was certainly not lost upon those who were able to observe them at first-hand. An Anglo-Saxon poem called 'The Ruin', written in the eighth century, quite possibly by a monk, almost certainly describes the scene in Bath as it then was:

Wondrous is this masonry, shattered by the Fates. The fortifications have given way, the buildings raised by giants are crumbling. The roofs have collapsed; the towers are in ruins. . . .

There is rime on the mortar. The walls are rent and broken away, and have fallen undermined by age. The owners and builders are perished and gone, and have been held fast in the earth's embrace, the ruthless clutch of the grave, while a hundred generations of mankind have passed away. Red of hue and hoary with lichen this wall has outlasted kingdom after kingdom, standing unmoved by storms. The lofty arch has fallen. . . . Resolute in spirit he marvellously clamped the foundations of the walls with ties. There were splendid palaces and many halls with water flowing through them; a wealth of gables towered aloft. . . .

And so these courts lie desolate, and the framework of the dome with its red arches sheds its tiles . . . where of old many a warrior, joyous hearted and radiant with gold, shone resplendent in the harness of battle, proud and flushed with wine. He gazed upon the treasure, the silver, the precious stones, upon wealth, riches and pearls, upon this splendid citadel of a broad domain. There stood courts of stone, and a stream gushed forth in rippling floods of hot water. The wall enfolded within its bright bosom the whole place which contained the hot flood of the baths. . . . (N. Kershaw, *Anglo-Saxon and Norse Poems*, Cambridge University Press, 1922.)

All the elements described by the poet are supported with remarkable precision by the archaeological evidence. Here is, without doubt, a dramatic eye-witness account of the Roman town in its death throes. By the eighth century enough of the superstructure, less the vaults, was still standing to be intelligible to the Anglo-Saxon poet, but by the eleventh century most of the old structure had probably disappeared, perhaps as the result of late Saxon builders removing suitable stone for re-use in the building programmes that were being undertaken at this time.

While it is true to say that the baths and temple had ceased to function in the manner for which they were built after the beginning of the fifth century, the same does not necessarily apply to the other buildings in the settlement, which were unaffected by problems of flooding. The house in Abbeygate Street, already described, continued to be occupied for a considerable period of time after the nominal end of Roman Britain in 410 and there is no reason to suppose that this was atypical. Town life in some form or another must have continued until, by 973, Bath had emerged as a town important enough to stage the coronation of King Edgar.

The processes which brought about the decline and re-emergence can be reconstructed, if only in broad outline, partly on the evidence from Bath itself and partly on analogy with sites in other parts of the country. In general terms the early fourth century was a period of prosperity for the towns and villa-owners, and even the peasant classes seem to have shared in the general affluence. Specialist schools of mosaicists could now be supported on the patronage offered by the rich, many of whom, like the owner of the Newton-St-Loe villa, were able to employ a team, probably based on Cirencester, whose speciality was the design and laying of figured mosaics depicting the Orpheus legend. But gradually, as the middle of the century approached, signs of the impending breakdown began to become noticeable. Manpower was in short supply, reflecting a decline in the birth rate, and consequently restrictive laws were passed to prevent the free movement of workers from one job to another. Tax burdens and the expensive responsibilities of public service were also making their effect felt in most areas, particularly the urban centres, but in spite of all this there was a sustained affluence which showed itself in the expensive alterations to the baths which continued to be made throughout the fourth century.

More serious than the purely economic factors were the threats from barbarian raiders, particularly the Picts and the Scots, which grew in their intensity until finally, in 367, the great 'Barbarian Conspiracy' launched a series of concerted raids on Britain. Picts, Scots, Franks, Saxons, Attocotti and Irish, aided by a disgruntled peasantry and certain rebellious elements in the army, managed to cause chaos as far south as the Thames. The country was in a state of anarchy. But the raiders had come to plunder for wealth and slaves, with no intention of military take-over or settlement. This is why when, two years later, Count Theodosius landed at Richborough with his army, he was unopposed, and by means of coercion and bribery, was able to restore the situation to order without undue delay.

The restoration which Theodosius engineered was thorough. The frontiers of both land and sea were put into order again by re-garrisoning Hadrian's Wall and by reorganizing, with extensions, the so-called Saxon Shore defences. The administrative machinery was supported and strengthened when necessary and, apparently for the first time, the towns were turned into strongly fortified bases from which a militia could spring into action if needed. The evidence for this is twofold: many of the towns with early third-century walls were strengthened at about this time by the addition of forward-projecting bastions fronted by a wide flat-bottomed ditch, the bastions to support war-machines such as ballistae and catapults, the ditch to keep any would-be attackers within the optimum killing range. Where towns or settlements were not already walled, such as Mildenhall, some kilometres east of Bath, a wall complete with attached bastions was built afresh. Although the dating evidence for each individual site is often vague, if it is correct to assume that these new works were all part of a unified scheme, the best context consistent with the available archaeological facts would be the Theodosian restoration. The second interesting piece of evidence is the occurrence of a distinct class of military fittings, usually of bronze, from forts and towns in southern Britain. It has recently been shown that these are of Germanic inspiration and probably represent equipment used either by the soldiers brought to Britain by Theodosius or by mercenaries from north Europe imported for the purpose of defending the towns. However this material is interpreted, its very existence, together with the modified defences, leaves little doubt that many of the towns had now become strongly fortified entities protected by resident troops.

It is not yet possible to say how Bath fitted into this pattern, although the uncertainty about the date of the town wall leaves open the possibility that it was not built until the late fourth century. Nor is it known whether the town was ever provided with bastions. The earliest town map, dating to about 1570, shows a series of bastions in some detail attached at intervals to all sides of the circuit, but it is very diagrammatic and the total absence of bastions on any of the later town maps, even that produced only forty years later by Speed, is puzzling. Either the early cartographer allowed himself considerable artistic licence or the defences had been completely modified during the Elizabethan period. It seems very unlikely, however, that a town in such a strategic position would have been left unprotected while others on lesser sites were now defended.

The events of 369 and the immediately following years were the last time that the central Roman government concerned itself directly with the affairs of the province. Thereafter Britain took care of itself by appointing a series of military commanders of varying degrees of competence, whose one ambition seems to have been to win a major battle on the Continent, in theory to protect Britain but usually to make a bid for the throne. To this end one army after another was amassed in the province only to be carried off to fight abroad, eventually to fail and be dispersed. By 409 there can hardly have been more than a handful of fighting men left. The countryside was in a state of turmoil, certain sectors of the community – quite possibly the peasants – having rebelled against the administrators and thrown them out, setting up 'a state of their own' as the writer Zosimus says. Then in 410 the final blow came: the Emperor Honorius, replying to a letter asking for help, firmly told the towns to look after their own defences. Britain was now on its own.

What followed is obscure but one thing stands out: many of the towns did survive as working entities. Even so, with government now fragmented and in the hands of tyrants and with the complex economic system of the Roman period in ruins, forcing society back into a state of bartering, the vitality of the cities was wasted. At best the surviving urban communities should be regarded as parasites on the carcase of the Roman achievement.

The sub-Roman leaders were faced with the threat of attack from most of the old enemies whom Theodosius had driven away forty years earlier. Two opposed policies were immediately favoured. Ambrosius wished to renew ties with the Roman armies who were still struggling on the Continent, whilst Vortigern supported the idea of continuing to bring in Saxon mercenaries, settling them in coastal regions as a kind of yeomanry to protect the land from amphibious raiders. To begin with Vortigern's policies prevailed but not without opposition, which caused him to build up his mercenary support. In about 442 the inevitable happened, the Saxon settlers rebelled and swept across the south and east in a series of plundering raids in which their relations from the homeland soon joined. Gildas, writing about a hundred years after, describes the event in vivid if rather exaggerated terms:

> For the fire of vengeance, justly kindled by former crimes, spread from sea to sea, fed by the hands of our foes in the east, and did not cease, until, destroying the neighbouring towns and lands, it reached the other side of the island, and dipped its red and savage tongue in the western ocean. . . . So that all the columns were levelled with the ground by the frequent strokes of the battering ram, all the husbandmen routed, together with their bishops, priests, and people, whilst the sword gleamed, and the flames crackled around them on every side. Lamentable to behold, in the midst of the streets lay the tops of lofty towers, tumbled to the ground, stones of high walls, holy altars, fragments of human bodies, covered with livid clots of coagulated blood, looking as if they had been squeezed together in a wine-press; and with no chance of being buried save in the ruins of the houses, or in the ravening bellies of wild beasts and birds. . . . (J. E. W. Wallis, *The Welding of the Race*, G. Bell & Sons, 1924.)

Needless to say, the rebellion marked the end of Vortigern's proSaxon policy and with the east of Britain now under Saxon domination the centre of the resistance moved to the west.

Whether the raiders reached the neighbourhood of Bath, it is impossible to say. There are some signs of disorder in the area, such as the burning down of the villa at Box and the bodies tipped down the well of the North Wraxall villa, but both of these events probably belonged to earlier troubles. In Bath itself the severed head of the girl thrown into the oven of the house in Abbeygate Street could well belong to the 440s, but precise dating is entirely lacking. However far the war bands had penetrated, they seem soon to have returned to the eastern areas and left the west to the control of the shadowy sub-Roman war leaders such as Ambrosius and Arthur. Soon after the rebellion had subsided, in about 446, an appeal for help was made to the Roman general Aetius: 'the Barbarians drive us to the sea, the sea drives us to the Barbarians. Between the two means of death we are either slaughtered or drowned.' Another over-statement and one, it seems, to which there was no response.

The next fifty years saw a period of raids and battles but the west maintained successful independence, winning a number of cavalry victories over their Saxon opponents, culminating in the famous victory at Mount Badon in about A.D. 500. After this, Gildas could speak of the present security but, he goes on, 'neither to this day are the cities of our country inhabited as before but being forsaken and overthrown, still lie desolate'.

By the middle of the sixth century the Saxon advance had gained a new impetus and eventually in 577 at the Battle of Dyrham in the Cotswolds, some kilometres to the north of Bath, the Saxons won a decisive victory, gaining the three towns of Bath, Cirencester and Gloucester. That the towns are mentioned at all is some indication that they were considered to be of importance, but what shreds of town life the Saxons inherited, it is impossible yet to say.

9

PRESENT AND
FUTURE

This book has been concerned with Bath in the distant past and with the way in which our knowledge of the period has developed over the last five centuries. It is important now to stand away from 'backward looking curiosity' in an attempt to understand the archaeological past in terms of the present and the future. It is right that societies should wish to understand their roots: a perspective of the past and a feeling of change and continuity are deep-seated human needs which should require no justification. That 700,000 people a year visit the baths is a fair reflection of the point and with the gradual increase in leisure time the numbers will inevitably rise out of all proportion. Those who bother to visit ancient monuments are becoming increasingly sophisticated in their demands. Attitudes of mild wonder are giving place to a more questioning and involved approach, resulting perhaps from the greater use made of archaeology in schools, as well as a much better visual presentation by the mass media, particularly television. The superficial romance of the subject is now, mercifully, being replaced by widespread informed interest.

If it is accepted that the presentation of archaeological material

is providing an increasing proportion of the community with a leisure and semi-leisure pursuit of positive intellectual worth (so it can
be argued, but not here), then it is clear that the attitude of society
to the physical remains of its past must necessarily take account of
this. There are two broad aspects to the problem: on the one hand
discovery and preservation, on the other, presentation and
communication.

Bath has been particularly fortunate in the attitude which the
civic authorities have taken towards its principal monuments in the
past. The excavations of the baths from 1878–96 were soon partially
displayed and additional areas were added to those open to the public
following the excavations of 1923. Now a total of 3,000 sq. m of
original Roman floor area is readily visible with the minimum of
encumbrance. But the public do not generally realize that nearly
another 1,000 sq. m of the most superb baths and hypocausts, quite
unparalleled in the country, lie beneath the streets to the west and
south and it is easily within the realms of possibility to clear the clutter
and open them up, thus making the entire bathing establishment once
more available to visitors as it has not been for 1,500 years.

The city fathers of the 1880s were far-sighted enough to see
that an investment in the Roman baths, allowing them to be seen
and appreciated by millions of visitors, was very much in the interests
of the city in that, by encouraging tourists, it ensured the community's prosperity. It is particularly satisfying to be able to record
that their successors, a century later, were bold enough to take a similar view when presented with a scheme to excavate and display a
substantial part of the temple precinct. The excavations of 1981–3
have brought thousands to Bath to watch the work in progress and
numbers continue to rise now that the excavations are on permanent
display. Nowadays investment in one's heritage is both educationally
desirable and financially wise.

Apart from the possibilities of display offered by the central
monuments, Bath poses a number of other archaeological questions
similar to those faced by excavators working in other towns – problems of ancient town planning, the social and economic development

of the site, the history of its defences and so on. But Bath has its own peculiarities. The ancient walled area, for example, is almost totally devoid of open spaces in which research excavations could be undertaken, while most of the standing buildings are of considerable architectural merit, and redevelopment, where it happens at all, is piecemeal and usually on a very small scale. The only policy to be adopted in these circumstances is one of watchful patience, making full use of each new building development as it arises to fill in the missing details. The scraps of evidence produced in this way will be as useful to future generations of archaeologists as those recorded by the antiquaries of the past have been to us.

This book, like any book on an archaeological aspect of a town, is essentially an interim summary. It attempts no more than to pinpoint the present state of our knowledge. Many seemingly isolated facts have been brought together to form a tolerably cohesive picture of a number of the more important monuments, and already it is possible to see them against the background of an evolving community, but this is really only the beginning.

At the time of writing schemes for redevelopment abound. The rebirth of the spa is imminent and with this will go the opportunity to study the Cross Baths and the Hot Bath spring and to excavate a large area immediately west of the temple precinct. At the same time there are proposals to develop semi-derelict land south of the baths. In all of these projects archaeologists will work hand in hand with developers. Who knows what will be found.

BATH AND BOOKS

Every town has its literature but few towns outside London have appeared as often as Bath has in literature. However, it is not the function of this book to review Bath in fiction from Chaucer to Jane Austen, but to indicate a selection of the more factual accounts of the town and its buildings.

Among the earliest general accounts it is difficult to better *The Itinerary of John Leland* (ed. Hearne, 1711), from which substantial sections have been quoted in the chapters above. The works of the topographers who followed Leland, though largely derivative, add many fascinating details. William Camden's *Britannia* (first edition, London, 1586) and William Stukeley's *Itinerarium Curiosum* (1723) are well worth consulting, the latter if only to see Stukeley's delightful prospect of the town in the early eighteenth century, before the great expansion. The first substantial account of the town itself was written by the architect John Wood and published in 1749 as *An Essay Towards A Description of Bath*, 'wherein', claims the title page, one will find a description of 'its Devastations and Restorations in the Days of the Britons, Romans, Saxons, Danes and Normans [and] its additional Buildings down to the end of the Year 1748'. The book is long, cumbersome but delightful. As an insight into the character of the man who did so much to transform the town which he so evidently loved, it is essential reading.

Much has been written on the architecture of the town, but Bryan Little's book *The Buildings of Bath* (Collins, 1947) and Walter Ison's *The Georgian Buildings of Bath* (Faber & Faber, 1949) together provide an easily accessible introduction to the subject to which we may now add Charles Robertson's *Bath: an Architectural Guide* (Faber & Faber, 1975) and a splendid illustrated corpus of Bath topographical prints, compiled by James Lees-Milne and David Ford, entitled *Images of Bath* (Saint Helena Press, 1982). For a view of the social life of the spa in its heyday, Edith Sitwell's *Bath* (Faber & Faber, 1932) is incomparable. A. Barbeau's *Life and Letters at Bath in the XVIIIth Century* (1904) offers more variety while R. S. Neale's *Bath: a Social History 1680–1850* (Routledge & Kegan Paul, 1981) gives a balanced scholarly account of the misery as well as the elegance.

It is difficult to choose from the quantity of contemporary derivative verbiage a true reflection of Victorian Bath. H. W. Freeman's *The Thermal Bath of Bath* (1888), a rather nasty piece of Victorian book production, comes perhaps closest to the true climate. It is a typical 'paste and scissors' work, but its gruesome accounts of diseases and specialist treatments, e.g. 'Gout and its Surgical Relations to the Human Economy', provide an insight into the social and architectural development of the city which is lacking in the more genteel *Northanger Abbey*.

Turning now to the more strictly archaeological literature, it is fair to say that until the middle of the eighteenth century the antiquities of Bath had usually been considered only in general itineraries or corpora, but with the discovery of the Roman baths during the building of the Duke of Kingston's Bath in 1755, specialized literature began to emerge. Dr Sutherland devoted six pages of his pamphlet *Attempts to Revive Ancient Medical Doctrine* (1763) to a first-hand account of the remains. The Pump Room discoveries of 1790 produced a spate of reports. Englefield's 'Account of Antiquities Discovered in Bath, 1790' was published in *Archaeologia* in 1792, a journal produced by the Society of Antiquaries, and a year later Governor Pownall issued a pamphlet, *Description of Antiquities dug up in Bath in 1790*, covering the same ground but including several additional finds. But all previous descriptions were made obsolete by the magnificent first volume of Samuel Lysons's *Reliquiae Romano Britannicae* (1813) which sets out for the first time a full and brilliantly illustrated corpus of all the inscriptions and sculptures found in Bath up to 1790. The book is a landmark not only in printing, but also in archaeological recording.

During the first half of the nineteenth century little more was found and original publications are correspondingly few. A few additions were made to the plan of the Baths in J. H. Spry's *Practical Treatise on the Bath Waters* (1822), but that was all. By the middle of the century, however, archaeological interest and archaeological publication were together growing fast: new national and county journals began to appear to report the spate of new discoveries. In Bath the Reverend H. M. Scarth published several papers. 'On Roman Remains Discovered in Bath' appeared in the third volume of the new *Proceedings of the Somerset Natural History and Archaeological Society* (1852). In Vol. V, two years later, Scarth's 'On Ancient Sepulchral Remains Discovered in and around Bath' was printed. In 1857, and again in 1861, he contributed notes 'On Roman Remains at Bath' to the *Journal of the British Archaeological Association* (Vols XIII and XVII), and in 1863 'On Roman Remains found on the site of the New Building added to the Bath Mineral Water Hospital in 1859' was published in the eleventh volume of the county journal. His major work, a rather unsatisfactory and badly produced compendium on Roman remains in and around Bath, was published under the title *Aquae Solis* in 1864.

The great period of discovery, 1867–96, has left remarkably little literature, but out of the growing awareness of antiquarian interest in the town sprang two local journals: *Proceedings of the Bath Field Club*, which first appeared in 1867 and lasted until 1904, and *Proceedings of the Bath and District Branch of the Somerset Archaeological Society*, which spanned the period 1904–42. These volumes are full of notes and reports, together with accounts of the field outings and lectures which the members suffered. Apart from the value of the original material published, the volumes are of enormous interest for the insight they provide into the concerns and aspirations of the amateur archaeological society of the day, out of which the modern archaeological structure of this country has grown.

Of the more important papers published during the main period of discovery we have J. T. Irvine's 'Remains of the Roman Temple and Entrance Hall to the Roman Baths found in Bath in 1790' in the *Journal of the British Archaeological Association*, Vol. XXIX (1873) and a note of the excavations of 1880–1 published in Vol. XXXVIII (1882) of the same journal. Irvine's main contribution, however, lay in his thorough manuscript notes on all the work with which he was concerned, which are now preserved in the Bath Reference Library. Richard Mann, the local builder employed throughout much of the time, published only a short note on the Roman culvert in the same journal, Vol. XXXIV (1878), but soon after 1900 he completed a set of superb drawings of all the major discoveries: these are now in the library of the Society of Antiquaries. The man responsible for the excavations, Major Charles Davis, was somewhat lax at objective archaeological reporting. He described the tin mask, found in a culvert, in a note in *Proceedings of the Society of Antiquaries of London* (Vol. VII, 1878) and on 24 June 1880 he read a paper to the Society concerning the excavation of the reservoir. The unpublished manuscript is now in the Society's library. Apart from this and a summary note in the *Bath Field Club* (Vol. LV, 1881) he wrote a fuller account of the early stages of the excavation entitled 'On the Excavations of the Roman Baths at Bath', which was first published in the *Transactions of the Bristol and Gloucestershire Archaeological Society* (Vol. VIII, 1884) and was later reprinted several times under the title *The Excavations of the Roman Baths at Bath*. Unfortunately the work is more an attack on his critics and a self-justification than a piece of unbiased archaeological writing. This somewhat sad chapter was, however, brought to a happy ending by the publication, in 1906, of the first volume of the *Victoria County History of Somerset*, in which Francis Haverfield brought together in a masterly synthesis the results of the previous two centuries' work.

Apart from minor discoveries which continued to appear in local journals, little happened until 1926 when W. H. Knowles published in *Archaeologia* (Vol. LXXV) his account of the east baths which he had excavated following the removal of the Duke of Kingston's Baths in 1923. This work marks the beginning of modern archaeological reporting. It was followed in 1955 by Professors Richmond and Toynbee's article 'The Temple of Sulis-Minerva at Bath' published in the *Journal of Roman Studies* (Vol. XLV), the first attempt to bring the temple, as a piece of social art history, to the attention of European scholars.

The quickening pace of modern development in the late 1950s and the institution of a Bath Excavation Committee in 1963 led to a series of rescue excavations of which the first, an excavation near the Southgate, was published by W. Wedlake in the county journal (Vol. CX, 1966). In the same year the present writer contributed a short account of the temple excavations of 1964–5 to *Antiquity* (Vol. XL, 1966). A detailed report on all the excavations from 1963–8, together with a reconsideration of the other buildings of the Roman city, was published as a research report of the Society of Antiquaries under the title *Roman Bath* (1969).

Since the first edition of this book was published a number of detailed archaeological reports have appeared, making available the results of excavations undertaken since 1969. *Excavations in Bath 1950–1975*, edited by the writer, includes a number of excavation reports and notes on various sites in the city, while my paper 'The Roman Baths at Bath: excavations 1969–75' published in the journal *Britannia* (Vol. VII for 1976) gives an account of the work undertaken at the west end of the baths when Major Davis's douche and massage baths were demolished. Elsewhere in the city Tim O'Leary carried out a rescue excavation on the defences at Upper Borough Walls the results of which were published in the journal *Medieval Archaeology* (Vol. XXV for 1981). An interim account of the excavation in the sacred spring in 1979, by the writer, appeared in *Antiquaries*

Journal (Vol. LX for 1980); the curses are being published annually as they are translated in the section entitled 'Roman Britain in 19—' in *Britannia* beginning in 1981. For the full publication of the recent excavations at the temple of Sulis Minerva we will have to wait for a year or two. Meanwhile this book offers the most up-to-date summary.

This expanded bibliography has been offered here in the hope that some readers may want to delve more deeply into aspects of the city's past. While no attempt has been made to list every reference, all the major accounts have been mentioned. I hope that those who begin to explore the literature will enjoy it as much as I have.

Index

INDEX

INDEX